TO MY FRIEND LISA-
BEST WISHES ALWAYS!

George Bugner

FRANCISCANOMICS

UPLIFTING STORIES FOR A DOWN ECONOMY

FRANCISCANOMICS
UPLIFTING STORIES FOR A DOWN ECONOMY

GEORGE BRYMER

ALL
SQUARE

All Square, Inc., Toledo, Ohio
© 2012 by George A. Brymer, Jr.
All rights reserved. Published 2012
Printed in the United States of America
21 20 19 18 17 16 15 14 13 12   1 2 3 4 5

ISBN-13: 978-0-9766335-0-1
ISBN-10: 0-9766335-0-7

Publisher's Cataloging-in-Publication *(Provided by Quality Books, Inc.)*

Brymer, George.
    Franciscanomics : uplifting stories for a down economy / George
Brymer.
        p. cm.
    Includes bibliographical references and index.
    LCCN 2011962587
    ISBN-13: 978-0-9766335-0-1
    ISBN-10: 0-9766335-0-7

    1. Recessions—History—21st century. 2. United
        States—Economic conditions—21st century.
        3. Generosity.   I. Title.

HB3717 2008.B79 2012   330.9'0511
                              QBI11-600237

This book is printed on recycled paper.

For Vicky

Contents

Acknowledgments

People often ask me how long it takes to write a book. In the case of *Franciscanomics,* the answer is fourteen months. Surprisingly, no one ever asks *how many people* it takes to produce a book.

If people did ask me that question, I'd first tell them about Laurel Marshfield. Laurel is an amazing editor who helps me where my writing needs it most—creating clear, reader-friendly transitions between my thoughts. A gifted author in her own right, Laurel understands the writing process—and the countless challenges that come with crafting a book. Her constant encouragement throughout this project, as well as her understated way of "holding my feet to the fire," made *Franciscanomics* a reality. I value her editorial insight, her fabulous sense of humor, and her friendship.

If anyone would ask, I'd also mention my friends Rob Davis and Amy Thomas, the two talented artists responsible for the book's cover. Rob designed the eye-catching dust jacket, and Amy drew the wonderful illustration of Saint Francis with the Wolf of Gubbio. I greatly appreciate their creative contributions.

I would also talk about the many remarkable people who agreed to be featured in *Franciscanomics*. These tireless individuals, who spend their days committing selfless acts, graciously made time to answer my questions. I'm honored to have the privilege of telling their extraordinary stories.

And, most of all, I would tell everyone about my wife, Vicky. It was her idea that I turn a short dinner speech called "Franciscanomics" into a book. But, then again, it's her steadfast love and support that inspires everything I do. And while I thank those who helped make *Franciscanomics* a better book, I thank Vicky for making me a better person. I dedicate this book—and, indeed, my life—to her.

George Brymer

FRANCISCANOMICS

UPLIFTING STORIES FOR A DOWN ECONOMY

Preface

A Recession's Silver Lining

In the spring of 2009, Shannon Polz, alumni relations officer for Lourdes University, asked me to speak at my alma mater's annual alumni dinner. At the time, the country seemed stalled in an unwavering economic recession, and Polz sensed that, like countless Americans, many Lourdes alumni felt dispirited by the lingering slump. So she hoped I could lift their moods with a speech focusing on the economy's positive aspects.

My reply, only half in jest, was, "What positive aspects?"

Americans, of course, had reason to be gloomy: employers were shedding hundreds of thousands of jobs each month; the auto industry was in a momentous slump; once-solid financial institutions were requiring government bailouts to stay afloat; and a sharp decline in the stock market had wiped out many people's retirement savings. Meanwhile, renowned economists were publicly debating whether the United States was experiencing its worst economic conditions since the 1930s.

What's more, several well-known corporations were embroiled in scandals involving falsified earnings statements, backdated stock options, poorly timed bonuses, and blatant mismanagement. This rash of disgraces added a troubling dimension to the recession: Americans were not only losing confidence in the financial system, but their trust in the very business leaders they counted on to orchestrate a recovery.

It was amid this grim economic news that Lourdes alumni officer Polz handed me the seemingly impossible task of discovering a silver lining and sharing it with my fellow alums.

A recent graduate myself, I was what college marketing directors call a *nontraditional* student—a description that, I suspect, is their euphemism for "old." To be sure, by the time I pursued my undergraduate degree at Lourdes, I had already witnessed numerous economic downturns during my thirty-year working career. Without a doubt, the most frightening economic crisis in my lifetime corresponded to Jimmy Carter's presidential term, a period during the late 1970s in which the country suffered the combined effects of high unemployment, skyrocketing interest rates, and double-digit inflation. My vivid memories of that debacle confirmed for me that, as bad as the current conditions appeared, things have indeed been worse. But while a history lesson might offer my audience some solace, it would hardly create the cheery post-dinner ambiance that Polz envisioned.

Fortunately, it was around this time that I began noticing random news stories about ordinary people who seemed to be weathering the recession by quietly doing good deeds. There was the major university's faculty who, though facing unpaid furloughs, chose to donate part of their salaries to protect the wages of their lower-paid co-workers. Then there was the bank CEO who made millions of dollars selling his majority stake in the company and—in a gesture uncharacteristic among today's greedy top executives—shared those proceeds with the hundreds of current and former employees whom he credited for his success. And there was the tech-savvy human resource consultant who found ways to use social media to help thousands of out-of-work strangers find jobs. Whereas news headlines were dwelling on economic misery and high-level corporate shenanigans, these uplifting stories received relatively little media attention.

So I decided to incorporate them in my speech as a way to counterbalance all the downbeat economic news. Besides, because of Lourdes' unique culture, I thought the alumni would find these stories especially meaningful.

Lourdes University, you see, is a Franciscan institution, by which I mean that its mission is deeply rooted in the values attributed to Saint Francis of Assisi. Toward that end, the Lourdes faculty and staff are dedicated to maintaining a community that's rich in learning, reverence, and service. Accordingly, I recognized a can't-miss-it similarity between Franciscan values and the motivation of those current-day unsung heroes—the charitable faculty members, the generous CEO, and the tweeting HR consultant—who, without fanfare, were making a difference in the world.

I thought it only logical, then, to include a reference to the university's beloved Saint Francis in my talk. Here I must confess that, like many of my former classmates, I knew little about the thirteenth-century evangelist on whose values Lourdes was founded. So I set about learning something about him that might prove relevant to my presentation.

Descriptions about Francis's exploits abound, and by most accounts, his was an unconventional—some may even say eccentric—life. The son of a wealthy textile merchant, Francis was born into privilege. Still, he was unusually sensitive to those in need, and although it earned him his friends' ridicule—and his father's wrath—Francis willingly shared his good fortune with local paupers. Of the many stories written about Francis, he is perhaps most celebrated for doing something unimaginable during the feudalistic era in which he lived: he renounced his father's riches and—devoting his life to spreading Christianity—chose to live in absolute poverty. Who in his right mind, many around him certainly must have wondered, would relinquish inherited wealth and status to undertake such a financially unrewarding task?

To that line of questioning, we could include this aforementioned foolishness: What reasonable college professors would forgo a week's salary *and* contribute to a relief fund for co-workers? For that matter, what practical-minded CEO would openly admit that his employees are the secret to his success, much less divvy up his stock profits among them? And, at a time when most people are knuckling down lest their own jobs be eliminated, what sensible HR professional would spend valuable time launching a social media campaign to help others find work? So illogical are these rare behaviors that we may consider them *Francis-like.*

In fact, these behaviors—framed by some highlighted realities of the economic recession and waning corporate integrity—became the basis for the twenty-minute speech I called "Franciscanomics." Afterwards, alumni diners were buzzing about Franciscanomics, already trying out the new word in their vocabularies. Many made a point to thank me for the heartening perspective on the economy. Polz shot me a grateful nod. And that was that.

Or so I thought.

Word of the speech soon made its way around campus. A few weeks later, Lourdes invited me to present it to the entire administrative staff. Then the alumni association's leadership branch recruited me to present "Franciscanomics" at its inaugural summit. The Association of Franciscan Colleges and Universities selected Franciscanomics as a breakout session for its 2010 symposium. Before long, companies and nonprofit organizations began hiring me to give the talk to their employees. Apparently, Franciscanomics was striking a chord among all who heard it.

But the question is, why?

The answer, I think, is that recessions make people weary. In other words, we grow tired of feeling helpless while waiting for another government stimulus bill, or the latest monetary policy shift to course-correct the economy. But in the meantime, the actions described in my speech are things *we* can do, and do right now. All that's necessary is for each of us to change our personal mindsets—to stop dwelling on our own hardships and begin focusing on helping others.

We also tire of feeling powerless to prevent gluttonous business leaders from expanding the modern-day feudalism that is increasingly widening the gap between the haves and have-nots. Franciscanomics behavior enables us to fight the onslaught of unethical leadership and show that people with Francis-like values still outnumber the corporate felons garnering so much publicity.

Unlike what its name may imply, Franciscanomics is not an economic theory. It's a simple lesson derived from the life of a humble man who chose sharing over hoarding, and put others before himself. This book—like the speech that inspired it—aims to demonstrate that lesson through stories about everyday people who are making those same choices.

You, too, may see an opportunity to make a tangible difference and join the Franciscanomics groundswell. Instead of being trapped in the mindset that our economic revival rests in the hands of ineffectual and hopelessly corrupt business leaders—those whose wealth and power actually seem to increase while others are struggling—you're free to embrace the realization that we are all responsible for producing a turnaround.

As Saint Francis realized, regardless of your present station in life—whether you're a college professor or a cafeteria worker, a bank president or a front-line teller, an HR consultant or a frustrated job seeker—we are all interdependent. For this reason, anything you do to make a difference in your own or other people's lives affects all of us. And by all of us, I mean the entire world.

Introduction

Shattered Faith and Renewed Hope

On Massachusetts Avenue in the Boston inner suburb of Cambridge, a short walk from Harvard University, are the offices of a private research organization known as the National Bureau of Economic Research. The NBER lists some of the country's most prominent economists among its members, including acclaimed scholars, Nobel Prize winners, and presidential advisors. For the better part of a century, the nonpartisan agency has been studying the effects of current and future government policies on the nation's economy.[1]

The Bureau's Business Cycle Dating Committee is a seven-member subgroup charged with ascertaining the dates that economic phases begin and end—or in an economist's vernacular, pinpointing the *peaks* and *troughs* of economic cycles. Formed in 1978, the committee has determined the beginning and ending dates of every economic cycle, all the way back to 1854.[2]

In early April 2010, the committee's members gathered at the NBER headquarters to identify the ending date for the recession that began in December 2007. For several months, favorable indicators had led many experts to publicly declare the recession over, prompting the committee to convene for the purpose of establishing exactly when the recovery began. But after careful deliberation, the committee made a surprising announcement: it was too early to pronounce the recession officially over.[3]

The "Great Recession"

It's understandable that economists would struggle to proclaim an end to the lingering downturn; after all, not since the Great Depression has a U.S. recession lasted so long.[4] And in the memories of some Americans, no previous recession has been as severe.

Yet it was almost totally, many experts contend, the fallout from a seemingly insignificant event, a *housing bubble*.[5] Emboldened by their confidence in this country's real estate market—specifically, their certainty that housing prices would continue to increase at historic rates—and driven by their unappeasable greed for profits, banks and mortgage companies began relaxing home-loan credit standards in the late 1990s. By granting so-called *subprime mortgages*, the bankers convinced themselves, they were putting homeownership within the reach of more Americans. Meanwhile, the easy access to credit created a seller's market that drove home prices to stratospheric heights.

But there was a catch. Many of the subprime loans included variable interest terms that permitted lenders to adjust rates after an initial period. Not surprisingly, when their mortgage interest rates increased, cash-strapped borrowers faced steeper monthly payments than they could afford. Consequently, the buyer demand that had inflated home prices quickly dried up, and housing prices plummeted 30 percent.[6] Mortgage lenders and their investors were left with insufficient collateral to cover the souring loans. The housing bubble had burst, thrusting the country's financial system into a dangerous liquidity crisis.[7]

When the housing bubble burst, the nation's banks faced a dire liquidity crisis.

In the months that followed, all hell broke loose. By the end of 2008, 12 percent of American mortgage holders were either behind in their payments or already in foreclosure. Once-solid mortgage institutions Fannie Mae and Freddie Mac, who held or secured more than half the outstanding home loans in the country between them, had to be rescued by the federal government.[8]

But it was not just mortgage lenders that were in trouble. Automakers General Motors and Chrysler filed for bankruptcy, prompting the U.S. Treasury to invest $81 billion to prevent a complete collapse of the domestic automotive industry—and making American taxpayers major shareholders in both companies.[9] Giant investment banker Lehman Brothers went bankrupt, and several other prominent financial institutions, teetering on the brink of extinction, required government intervention in order to stay in business. American Insurance Group, once the country's largest insurance company, received $165 billion in government aid. Meanwhile, the feds hastily brokered deals in which Bank of America purchased a failing Merrill Lynch and J.P. Morgan bought Bear Stearns at a fire-sale price. The Treasury established the Troubled Asset Relief Program, or TARP, and ultimately spent billions transferring questionable loans from the books of struggling lenders to the federal government's own balance sheet.[10] Over the next two years, despite efforts like TARP, banking regulators shut down record numbers of insolvent banks and thrifts; by mid-2010, one in ten U.S. banks was at risk of failing.[11]

Eager to avert an economic catastrophe, Congress approved an $800 billion economic stimulus plan in early 2009.[12] But Americans were already feeling the recession's toll. In March that same year, the Dow Jones Industrial Average closed at 6,763—a 52 percent drop from its October 2007 peak.[13] Wall Street's extraordinary collapse wiped out many people's savings, postponing the retirements of some workers, and leaving others to wonder if they could ever afford to retire.

Not that work was easy to find. The unemployment rate doubled from 5 percent at the start of the downturn to 10.1 percent in October 2009, and it continued to hover near double-digit territory throughout the recession.[14] By the summer of 2010, almost half of unemployed workers had been jobless for over six months.[15] What's more, nearly twice as many U.S.

workers were underemployed—that is, they either lacked a job altogether or were working part-time while seeking full-time employment. And among those who were working, many lived in fear of losing their jobs, having their wages cut, or getting fewer hours.[16]

Just when improving corporate earnings reports—and an upward-creeping stock market—gave indications that the worst might be over, financial turmoil in Europe dashed hopes that a global recovery was underway.[17] Problems overseas, along with lingering high unemployment at home, sent the U.S. economy into further retreat—leading to what some economists called a *double-dip* recession.[18]

Coining a term that compared current conditions to the Great Depression, former Federal Reserve Chair Paul Volcker proclaimed, "The U.S., along with the rest of the world, is in the midst of a great recession."[19]

Recession-weary Americans received an added mental jolt in September 2010. Five months after failing to determine an ending date for the recession, the NBER's Business Cycle Dating Committee reconvened. After analyzing such bellwether indicators as gross domestic product and gross domestic income, the members agreed that the economy had bottomed out in June 2009. In other words, according to the brightest economic minds in the country, the recession had been over for fifteen months.[20] The committee's announcement brought little comfort to the countless Americans who remained out of work, faced foreclosure on their homes, or had postponed retirement indefinitely. On the contrary, the fact that the nation's foremost financial experts considered the recession over left many people with the impression that our leading authorities were out of touch with economic reality, and added to an overwhelming sense of hopelessness.[21]

While conventional measurements may have signaled that a recovery was underway, one thing was abundantly clear: the timetables prescribed by academic models and economic formulas would not constrain the "Great Recession." For most Americans, the recession—while technically over—was still wreaking havoc.

Are We Better Off Now?

Many of the country's most prominent financial authorities have predicted that the Great Recession will go down as the worst economic cycle since the 1930s.[22] But those Americans who endured the economic adversity that coincided with the Carter Administration would likely disagree.[23]

A review of interest rates in 1980, the final year of Carter's single-term presidency, supports the argument that those were harder times. That year, the U.S. prime rate soared to 21.5 percent, its highest point in history.[24] Mortgage rates were in the mid teens. By comparison, the prime rate actually went down during the Great Recession, reaching a rock bottom 3.25 percent in December 2008, and remaining there for the duration. Meanwhile, average rates on thirty-year fixed-rate mortgages also dropped, falling below 4.5 percent in 2010, their lowest level in fifty years.[25]

The exorbitant interest rates during President Carter's term meant that companies could not afford to borrow money, which prevented many from running their plants or operating their factories. As a result, supplies of consumer goods dried up, and as dictated by the law of supply and demand, prices skyrocketed. The U.S. inflation rate hit a staggering 14.76 percent in March 1980.[26]

Question:
Is this the worst
economy since the
Great Depression?

Without goods to produce, companies laid off workers in droves. Unemployment reached 7.8 percent in 1980. But the wreckage of the Carter economy would continue to cause joblessness for years to come, and the unemployment rate hit 10.8 percent before leveling off in 1982.[27]

From an average American's standpoint, one way to compare the Great Recession to 1980 conditions is through the *misery index,* a simple but telling formula conceived by the late economist Arthur Okun. This Brookings Institute scholar invented the misery index during the 1970s. The monthly computation involves adding the unemployment and inflation rates together.[28] Although the Great Recession brought high unemployment, inflation remained virtually nonexistent; as a result, the misery index varied from a low of -2.10 to a high of 5.60. But back in June 1980, just in time for President Carter's re-election campaign, the misery index reached an all-time high of 21.98.

Consequently, in Ronald Reagan's own 1980 run for the presidency, all he had to do was point out the obvious: Americans were economically miserable. In a nationally broadcast debate a week prior to the election, Reagan asked viewers to consider, "Are you better off than you were four years ago?"[29] Voters answered with a resounding "no" and swept Reagan into office with an electoral landslide.[30]

So while politicians will always disagree about the country's economic well-being from one administration to the next, history proves that, on paper at least, conditions are better today than they were in the late 1970s and early 1980s.

Having said that, the era surrounding the Great Recession does have an unusual feel to it. Indeed, there's an added dimension to this downturn. While our corporations are still producing more than enough goods, there's evidence that *leadership integrity* is in short supply. And for that reason, it's not just our confidence in the financial system that is crumbling, but also our faith in the leaders who run the powerful institutions of our country.

American Feudalism

In his address to St. Anselm College's class of 2002, a prominent commencement speaker had a timely warning for graduates about the ethical challenges awaiting them in the workplace. "You will be confronted with questions every day that test your morals," he told the Manchester, New Hampshire audience. "Think carefully, and for your sake, do the right thing, not the easy thing."[31]

Sadly, that speaker, former Tyco International CEO Dennis Kozlowski, ignored his own good advice and chose to do the wrong thing instead. So, what he's "doing" now is eight to twenty-five years, his prison sentence for misappropriating hundreds of millions of dollars from the company's coffers.[32]

Kozlowski brazenly treated Tyco's bank accounts as if they were his own.[33] Company shareholders unwittingly financed Kozlowski's personal extravagances, including a $15 million vintage yacht, nearly $20 million in artwork, and a $2.1 million party in Sardinia to celebrate his wife's birthday. He spent $60 million of company funds on two lavishly furnished homes: a Boca Raton mansion and a Fifth Avenue apartment in Manhattan. Kozlowski also used company funds to make sizeable charitable donations, which he shamelessly claimed as his own; in one instance, he made a $5 million gift to Seton Hall University, which his alma mater acknowledged by naming a building after him—a building the school has understandably renamed since his conviction.[34]

> ## Americans began to realize that many corporations were not victims of the financial crisis, but contributors to it.

Although Kozlowski went to jail years before the Great Recession began, his conduct symbolizes a twenty-first century rash of criminal activity at the highest levels of corporate leadership. Still reeling from recent scandals at companies like Tyco, Enron, Arthur Anderson, and WorldCom, Americans spent much of the Great Recession trying to comprehend a new development in immoral business activity: the outrageously criminal.

Indictments against Citigroup, Bank of America, American Insurance Group, and Goldman Sachs charged executives with deliberately concealing their companies' subprime mortgage exposure from investors and customers.[35] The public quickly realized that those institutions, with their household names and reassuring marketing messages, were not victims of the financial crisis; they were perpetrators who took part in its creation. That realization fueled a universal perception that a growing number of corporate leaders share an *anything goes* mentality when it comes to making money.

But the blatantly illegal behavior of some top executives has only been outdone by the callous and stupid actions of the corporate elite. A case in point is American Insurance Group. Just days after receiving an $85 billion installment of their taxpayer-funded bailout, AIG's leaders audaciously spent $440,000 to pamper seventy key employees for an entire week at the opulent St. Regis Resort in California.[36]

And who can forget the chief executives of automakers General Motors, Chrysler, and Ford who traveled to Washington, D.C. seeking billions of dollars in federal assistance for their companies? The help was justified, the CEOs explained to a Senate committee, because it would keep their expense-laden organizations from filing bankruptcy and save millions of industry jobs. But to the astonishment of the committee members and the American public, the CEOs admitted to flying to Washington separately in their private company jets.[37]

Then there were BP's top executives, Carl-Henric Svanberg and Tony Hayward, who, after one of their company's offshore oil rigs exploded in the Gulf of Mexico, killing eleven workers and causing the largest environmental disaster in history, publicly uttered one insulting comment after another. Svanberg angered Gulf Coast residents when he told reporters, "We care about the small people." Complaining about the public relations burden the oil spill had caused him, Hayward—seemingly oblivious to the fact that several of his employees had lost their lives in the accident—lamented, "I would like my life back."[38]

Business scandals, of course, are nothing new. But there is a broad perception that appalling leadership behavior is suddenly on the rise. Wharton ethicist Thomas Donaldson offers one explanation: economic downturns help unveil the types of corporate misconduct that are easily obscured during periods of enormous growth. For instance, it took the bursting of the housing bubble to reveal how large financial institutions had intentionally concealed their overexposure to subprime mortgages. "As the level of the lake lowers," says Donaldson, "you start to see the wrecks as they come to be exposed."[39]

Other experts offer their own theories to explain the mounting ethical wreckage. Some analysts blame executive compensation plans that are heavily weighted in stock options and, as a result, encourage business leaders to exercise whatever-it-takes measures to manipulate their companies' share prices. Others point to innovations in financial tools for which ethical guidelines have yet to be established, as was the case with the complex vehicles used to sell subprime mortgages to investors. Many fault boards of directors who overlook improper behavior within their companies, either through negligence or complicity. Scariest of all explanations, perhaps, is that most business scoundrels don't even think that what they're doing is wrong.[40]

Whatever the reason for the increase, one thing is certain: in the wake of fraudulent activities, dim-witted decisions, and thoughtless remarks, our confidence in business leaders has been destroyed. That shattered faith is the added dimension to the Great Recession.

It's as if today's corporate chieftains, with their ill-gotten riches and barefaced disregard for society, have created a form of feudalism in America. Feudalism had its roots in medieval Europe, when wealthy aristocrats used their positions to extract labor from peasants, who in turn expanded the nobles' wealth and gave them even greater power.[41] Look closely and you'll see a striking similarity between feudal aristocracy and Tyco's embezzling ruler Dennis Kozlowski: he exploited his authority to create a personal fiefdom while the company's loyal subjects toiled for mere fractions of his outrageous earnings. Like the feudalists of the Middle Ages, a growing number of today's CEOs don't hesitate to treat themselves like royalty.

Our founding fathers rebelled against the feudalistic British monarchy. But unless we stand up to today's corporate tyranny, we will have come full circle, returning to a form of feudal, top-down rule. And while there's no need to take up muskets or assemble on the village green for battle, it is high time for a new kind of revolution.

Trickle-Down Theory

When Ronald Reagan became president, he applied an economic strategy called the *trickle-down effect* to repair the recession he inherited. Very simply put, trickle-down theory suggests that by easing costly regulations and lowering taxes on business investments, government will allow companies to flourish—and the resulting corporate profits will ultimately trickle down to lower-income individuals.[42]

> # Reaganomics preceded seven and a half years of continual economic growth.

Scholars have long disagreed about the overall effectiveness of trickle-down economics.[43] What's more, the concept provides fodder for philosophical debate—the very definition of trickle-down theory conjures up images of a feudalistic society in which hapless vassals are forced to live off the scraps of a few well-to-do corporate lords. And wasn't it the easing of banking regulations that accelerated the housing bubble's collapse? Nevertheless, during Reagan's administration, the trickle-down effect proved hugely successful in turning around a stagnant economy.

In fact, after the Carter recession finally ended in 1982, the U.S. economy experienced its longest period of peacetime growth in history: ninety-two consecutive months of sustained expansion. *Reaganomics,* as many would soon call the model, brought the country's unemployment and inflation rates back into line. On Wall Street, the Dow Jones Industrial Average nearly tripled during the 1980s. Reaganomics ushered in an age of unparalleled economic growth.[44]

Unfortunately, the economic momentum credited to Reaganomics didn't last forever. Near the turn of the century, reduced oversight of the mortgage industry helped drive an increase in subprime loans, inflated home prices, and a dangerous housing bubble. While the economy bounced between expected, cyclical highs and lows, the public had no reason to suspect that a colossal downturn was looming. Then, in December 2007, America entered a Great Recession.

But for many people, the Great Recession is more than just an economic slump. The fear that a full economic recovery remains a long way off is coupled with a deep disappointment that the very leaders who should be driving that recovery are lacking in both integrity and common sense.

So while current policy makers attempt to kick-start an economic recovery with textbook initiatives like stimulus packages, tax cuts, and infrastructure rebuilding programs, they'll also need a strategy for restoring the public's faith in the tarnished leaders who oversee the intricate workings of our economy.

But beyond what government officials may or may not do

to restore the economy and America's faith in the leadership class, more and more "ordinary" citizens are refusing to wait for an economic recovery to trickle down and save them. Instead, they are choosing to do whatever they can to stimulate a turnaround in their own and others' lives. In the process, they're rejecting the notion that their difficulties are isolated problems, and electing instead to embrace the view that all Americans are connected through common economic circumstances—that they, and we, are all in this together.

And when that happens, when we join forces to help each other deal with our economic burdens, our perspective on the Great Recession will be forever changed.

A Case Study

I know of one young man who came to see things that way. Epitomizing the stereotypes associated with members of Generation Y, this son of a wealthy textile magnate exemplified the sense of entitlement that many people readily attribute to today's youth. To be sure, trickle-down theory held special meaning for this flashy dude: his father's profits trickled down to him in the form of a generous allowance. He freely spent his money on fine clothes in the latest fashions and on lavishly entertaining his friends. And when it came time for him to find a job amid a tough economy, his dad simply put him to work in the family business.

On one fateful day, this fellow was hard at work in his father's retail shop. The store was busy with wealthy customers who had the financial wherewithal to make sizeable purchases.

Surely, he thought, he could please his father—and hopefully boost his allowance—by closing several large orders. Just then, a beggar wandered in from the street, approached the owner's son, and asked him for a handout. The unexpected confrontation embarrassed the young man in front of his customers (what might these affluent clients think of an establishment that attracts beggars?), so he abruptly told the vagabond to leave—turning him away empty handed.

Then it was his turn to beg—for forgiveness.

Returning to his customers, the shopkeeper's son could not stop thinking about his regrettable behavior toward the needy man. His reputation was that of a bighearted person, and he ordinarily would have gladly given the beggar some money. But on this occasion, his concern about offending the store's patrons—and his panic over losing some large sales—clouded his judgment. He wished he had acted differently.

Feeling remorse, the young man ran out of the store after his customers were gone to search for the beggar. He frantically stopped people on the street and asked if they had seen him, and although it took quite a while, he did finally locate the man. Then it was *his* turn to beg—for forgiveness. He apologized to the beggar for brushing him off in the store, and he gave him all the money he had in his pockets.[45]

At first glance, it would appear that the young man was simply practicing trickle-down economics that day, by sharing his earnings with someone in need. However, the incident would prove to be a milestone in his life—from that day on, his personal wealth held no value to him.

That story's subject was a man named Francis, who we today know as Saint Francis of Assisi. As we'll see, this anecdote reveals a basic human value—our willingness to help others—that is the one value that will steer us toward recovery.

The episode with the beggar did not go unnoticed by Francis's friends. They ridiculed him for what they considered a foolish waste of his money. And his father, who had no interest in charitable acts, was equally critical and ordered Francis to stop giving away his money.

Despite his friends' mockery and his father's scorn, Francis continued to find ways to employ his makeshift trickle-down methods. While praying in a local church one day, Francis heard the figure carved into the altar's crucifix speak to him: "Francis, go and repair my church, which, as you see, is falling into ruins." Looking around at the holes in the ceiling and crumbling stone on the walls, Francis assumed that God was telling him to spruce up the place.[46] Thus Francis began using some of the family's profits to help fix up the church.

When his father got word of how Francis was squandering his money, he confronted his son and demanded repayment. Francis refused and, there in the church, in the presence of his father and the bishop, renounced his family's riches. He preferred living in poverty to living with his father's selfishness. To underscore his decision, Francis disrobed and handed the clothes he'd been wearing—a symbolic last vestige of his par-

ents' support—to his astounded father. His easy access to
trickle-down resources was now behind him.

But as it turned out, patching the church was not what
Francis was being called to do. It was not a building that
needed repairing. No, his task was to restore the church in the
universal sense; that is, to rescue it from widespread corruption
and disbelief. It was to that duty and to helping others that
Francis devoted the remainder of his life. And in emulating his
example, Francis's many followers helped combat the oppressive feudalism that was prevalent in his lifetime.[47]

Ripple-Out Theory

So while we long for an end to the Great Recession, what
should *our* assignment be? Is it to rebuild the balances in our
401(k) accounts? Or is it something far greater? Perhaps our
job is to repair the public's faith that—in an age of corporate
greed and shameful, if not criminal, misconduct—there are
still principled people in the world.

There are those who would say that it's the government's
job to address the leadership crisis, along with the economic
upheaval. They assert that lawmakers must enact new and
tougher regulations, which mandate higher moral behavior
among business leaders. Opponents answer that the Sarbanes-
Oxley Act—legislation aimed at requiring proper behavior in
publicly traded corporations—went into effect in 2002, the
same year that Dennis Kozlowski delivered his hypocritical
commencement address, and long before the recent scandals
that this act was intended to prevent. Besides, mired in partisan

bickering and political posturing, the legislature can only do so much. No, waiting for government officials to impose ever more top-down solutions is not the answer.

But some may argue, "What can we do? It's not like we're saints."

Well, if the task seems overwhelming, consider this astonishing story of selfless generosity.

Facing $38 million in state funding cuts, officials at Clemson University made the gut-wrenching decision in 2009 to furlough every employee for five days without pay. Predictably, some faculty members promptly approached administrators to voice their concerns about the fairness of these furloughs. Officials were undoubtedly prepared for a certain amount of resistance. But imagine their surprise when they learned that their teachers weren't troubled by the effect on their own paychecks. They were instead worried about Clemson's lower-wage workers, those for whom a one-week pay cut could be devastating.[48]

Working with the faculty, Clemson officials established a relief fund to support employees who needed financial assistance to weather the furloughs. Faculty, staff, students, trustees, businesses, and the public donated more than $71,000 to the fund, and 158 employees received money to offset their forfeited income.[49]

You may be wondering how a relief fund differs from the concept of trickle-down economics. In both cases, those with means assist those without. Yet the trickle-down effect works because those at the top of the system receive an incentive for helping those at the bottom—a tax cut or fewer regulations, for example. But donors to the Clemson relief fund were not offered an enticement; they simply chose to help. Rather than inadvertently trickling their excesses down to their co-workers, the Clemson staff let their good fortune ripple out instead.

As more people follow Clemson's lead, our combined efforts will ripple outward—and create real change.

Ripple-out theory is not an actual economic premise, mind you. But the term accurately describes the actions of a growing number of compassionate people like those at Clemson. While trickle-down economics reflects a hierarchical order—with government and major corporations at the top and the American public on the bottom—ripple-out theory depicts a level playing field.

As more people follow Clemson's lead, our combined efforts will ripple outward. And together, all Americans—from whatever perch in the economy we happen to occupy—will begin to create real change.

Franciscanomics

How is the Clemson staff's behavior Francis-like? It's awfully easy to imagine that many of the university's faculty members, upon hearing about the furloughs for the first time, were initially struck by how the pay cut would affect them personally. That's human nature, after all; even Saint Francis's immediate reaction when confronted by the beggar in his father's shop was self-centered. And to our economic and emotional detriment, that kind of me-first reaction has been widely adopted in our culture.

But like Francis, the Clemson teachers quickly switched to a different mindset. In the middle of an economic recession, knowing that they would be losing a week's pay, Clemson faculty and staff members did not dwell on their own hardships; on the contrary, they shifted their concern to the furlough's impact on their co-workers. And like Francis, who ran into the street in search of the beggar he had turned away, they acted on their change of heart.

So if the I'm-only-in-it-for-myself philosophy being demonstrated by countless business executives is destroying your faith in people, take heart. The headlines might not reflect it, but stories like the Clemson initiative abound. In a manner reminiscent of Saint Francis, whose emotional connection with a beggar turned his socially sanctioned selfishness inside out, everyday people are undergoing similar transformations. Realizing that all of us are inextricably connected through the economy—in recessions as well as in periods of prosperity—they're proving that when we help others through tough times we also help ourselves.

In the spirit of a growing vocabulary of words formed by blending terms with *economics* (e.g., Reaganomics, *Freakonomics*), Franciscanomics is my name for a movement that's quickly gaining traction in our country. Across the United States people are quietly pitching in, doing whatever they can in remarkably kind and creative ways, to ease the Great Recession's devastating effects on those around them.

In *Franciscanomics,* you'll read about everyday Americans who exhibit a Francis-like mindset. I'll introduce you to Joe Works, a small-town business owner who's doing everything within his power to keep from laying off his employees. You'll meet movie producer and social entrepreneur Peter Samuelson, who's giving homeless people an alternative to sleeping in cardboard boxes. I'll tell you about Jorge Muñoz, a school bus driver in Queens, New York, who feeds dozens of hungry immigrant day workers hot meals—every single night. You'll learn how Becky Fawcett and her husband, parents of two adopted children, are using their financial resources to help other families afford the high cost of adoption. I'll also introduce Michele Armstrong, a Pennsylvania dog lover who's put together a dedicated army of volunteers to rescue doomed dogs from overcrowded animal shelters. And you'll read about many more people who are demonstrating the Franciscanomics philosophy.

You don't have to be religious to appreciate *Franciscanomics.* Indeed, this is not a book about religion. You only need to appreciate the compassionate values that Saint Francis demonstrated in his everyday actions. Nor do you need any special knowledge about economics; in fact, you've already learned all you need to know: the obvious difference between "trickle down" and "ripple out."

So let's get started. As you read this book, one fact should become clear: although a small group of greedy figures has cast a shadow on the entire business world, the actions of people like those described in *Franciscanomics* can restore us to the belief that people, in general, want to behave in ways that benefit the greater good of all.

One

A Job Angel and a Thoughtful Man

Residents of the Italian city of Gubbio were living in terror. A savage wolf was roaming the countryside, attacking and devouring animals and people alike. Those who ventured from town armed themselves as if they were going off to war; wise people avoided traveling altogether. Only one person dared to confront the beast. His name was Francis.

Saint Francis was living in Gubbio at the time, and he empathized with his fearful neighbors. So, as the legend goes, ignoring the prevailing advice against it, Francis set off to have a talk with the wolf.

When Francis came face-to-face with the ferocious animal, it leapt toward him "with gaping jaws." Francis made the sign of the cross while commanding the wolf to stay, and the fierce creature tamely bowed at his feet. After explaining to the wolf that his brutal behavior had caused Gubbio's citizens to fear and despise him, Francis offered the animal a deal: if the wolf would stop terrorizing the people of Gubbio, Francis would arrange for the townspeople to keep him fed. Nodding in agreement, the wolf gently laid his paw in Francis's hand as if the two were sealing their pledge with a handshake.[1]

From then on, the wolf and Gubbio's residents kept the pact that Francis had negotiated. Not only did people feel safe to travel outside the city again, they also welcomed the wolf into their town. When the animal died two years later, it wasn't his savage acts that people remembered most, but his role in helping Francis teach this lesson in kindness.

Since this book, *Franciscanomics,* is about the compassion of current-day heroes, it seems fitting for the Great Recession to serve as a metaphoric wolf. After all, there is nothing more frightening to many people than the thought of falling victim to the "gaping jaws" of unemployment.

The Great Recession is having a demoralizing effect on American workers.

During the Great Recession, U.S. employers slashed nearly eight million jobs.[2] Fifteen million Americans were unemployed in the fall of 2010. By the summer of 2011, 30 percent of the nation's jobless had been out of work for more than a year.[3] Furthermore, experts were forecasting that employment would not improve to pre-recession levels before 2013. One in two unemployed workers was without health insurance.[4] Many unemployed workers over the age of fifty were wondering if they would ever work again.[5]

Few Americans have escaped unemployment's vicious bite. Since the Great Recession began in December 2007, nearly three quarters of U.S. companies underwent some type of employee downsizing. Countless other employers, in their attempts to avoid layoffs, have frozen or reduced wages, eliminated overtime, imposed furloughs, increased workers' share of health care costs, and discontinued matching 401(k) contributions.[6] Meanwhile, fears that further job cuts are looming—not to mention the weariness of taking on the additional workloads of their laid-off co-workers—are causing even those employees whose jobs have been spared to feel helpless and sad.

So while being clutched in the jaws of recession continues to take a financial toll on companies, it's also having a demoralizing effect on the people who comprise America's workforce.

Question is, who among us will reason with the beast of unemployment and make us feel safe again?

The Job Angel

On a late-January morning in 2009, Mark Stelzner was eating breakfast at his home in the West End neighborhood of downtown Washington D.C., and thinking about unemployment. News from the labor market had been especially bleak that week, with officials reporting major job losses in every sector of the U.S. economy. The unemployment rate had reached 7.6 percent, its highest level in thirty-four years, and experts were predicting that joblessness would continue to escalate.[7]

Stelzner, a human resources consultant, had an inspiration that morning. He had been toying around on Twitter, the real-time social-networking website through which users exchange short messages called *tweets*. At the time, Stelzner had around 700 "followers"—Twitter lingo for people who regularly read his tweets—and, like him, many of his followers were HR professionals. What if, Stelzner wondered, he and his followers each helped an out-of-work person find a job?[8]

"You game?" tweeted Mark Stelzner.

So he tweeted about his idea: "Was thinking that if each of us helped just 1 person find a job, we could start making a dent in unemployment. You game?"[9]

You game? The response to his challenge was, as Stelzner puts it, "immediate and overwhelmingly positive." Before the morning was out, a grassroots effort was underway using social media to help people all over the country find jobs. Stelzner and his followers named their movement JobAngels, and in its very first year, over 40,000 "angels" began helping people land new positions.

Some job angels are passing along job leads or offering to make personal introductions to potential employers. Others are editing résumés or coaching jobseekers on how to handle interviews. And more often than not, they're helping complete strangers.[10] While the informal nature of social media makes tracking exact results difficult, Stelzner personally knows of over 1,650 people who have found work through JobAngels.[11]

Stelzner and his fellow job angels evoke the philosophy of Franciscanomics because they defy the wait-and-hope, trickle-down approach to joblessness. "It was one simple idea," says Stelzner, "that somehow tapped into people's desire to stop being victims to a seemingly endless stream of angst, depression, and relentless negativity."[12]

By making a collective effort to reduce unemployment, tens of thousands of job angels are demonstrating the Franciscanomics we're-all-in-it-together mindset. "For those who have joined the movement, I see a strong sense of camaraderie and common purpose," reports Stelzner. "This recession has touched everyone in some way, shape, or form, and despite our diversity, we share a common thread of wanting to get people back to work."[13]

It would be easy for us to imagine that helping people escape the jaws of unemployment is something that only saints and angels are cut out to do. But that is not the case.

Keeping the Wolf at Bay

In the town of Humboldt, Kansas—population: just under 2,000—one business owner is taking extraordinary steps to minimize the Great Recession's impact on his employees. Joe Works, whose company, B&W Trailer Hitches, employs nearly 10 percent of Humboldt's residents, is paying his idled workers to spruce up their community.[14]

If any company could justify employee layoffs during the Great Recession, B&W could. The company manufactures truck beds and trailer hitches, and the markets for both products are heavily dependent on the sales of new pickup trucks. With truck sales suffering from high gasoline prices and a slumping auto industry, B&W's revenues fell sharply soon after the downturn began. Works, the W in the B&W name, tried cutting hours and having his workers offset their lost wages by collecting unemployment benefits under the Kansas Shared Work program. Then, when the unemployment payments ran out, he paid some of his workers to remodel the plant's offices. But with the office transformation complete and orders still lagging, there wasn't enough work to keep all of B&W's 180 employees busy.

Not enough conventional work, that is. In a staff meeting one day, talk somehow turned to the rusted-out condition of the storm-sewer grates in downtown Humboldt. Bothered by the unsightliness of the drains, and looking for a way to keep from laying off unoccupied employees, Works assigned a handful of workers the task of fashioning new grates from the plant's scrap metal and installing them around town. From there, according to Works, he and his crew began imagining what other "random acts of kindness" they could do for the community.[15]

Employees completed the work while they were on the company clock.

As it turns out, they found plenty around Humboldt to keep the company's workers busy. Since that original endeavor of replacing the town's sewer grates, B&W employees with time on their hands have installed bleachers at the county fairgrounds, and replaced the roof on a park's shelter house.

They've refurbished tennis courts and, in a town that claims baseball greats Walter Johnson and George Sweatt as natives, constructed several ball diamonds. They've even performed maintenance projects on each other's homes. And all the work was completed while employees were on the clock, giving employees and their families the security that comes from having steady wages.

Reminiscent of Saint Francis, who used the family business's profits to repair the bricks and mortar of a decaying church, Works has responded to a similar call. It's probably just a coincidence, but B&W employees have painted and made other cosmetic touchups to all of Humboldt's cash-strapped churches. Whatever it was that moved him, Works is helping the town he loves make much-needed repairs.

At the same time, Works is doing his part to tame the recessionary wolf that threatens his employees. "A layoff would be troubling and stressful and financially difficult," says Works, "and seeing that there was a plan to avoid that provided some peace of mind."[16]

As it turns out, it's not just Humboldt's ball fields and shelter houses that Works is keeping in good repair; he's maintaining the spirit of the entire community. By helping his neighbors make over their city, Works hopes that B&W's efforts prove to be a supportive push in the right direction—the impetus to help revitalize this small rural town and give its residents renewed optimism. And if he has to dig into his own pocket to make it happen, so be it.

Nowhere is the one-for-all spirit of Franciscanomics more

vividly demonstrated than in Humboldt, Kansas, through the ripple-out efforts of Joe Works.

What Gives?

What is it that motivates people like Joe Works and Mark Stelzner to help others? What separates individuals like Works and Stelzner—people who take matters into their own hands—from those who'd rather let solutions trickle down from someone or something else?

Psychologists believe our desire to help others has something to do with empathy—more specifically, a human emotion known as *empathic distress.* Empathic distress is our individual reaction to someone else's physical, psychological, or economic suffering.[17] Simply put, news of someone else's misfortune arouses our own feelings of distress and, for a variety of possible motives, makes us want to lend a hand.

There's evidence suggesting that empathic distress is innate. In a study conducted in the mid-1970s, researchers exposed one-day-old infants born at University of Michigan Hospital to actual and simulated sounds of another baby crying. The newborns cried significantly more often to the cries of an actual baby than they did when exposed to computer-generated crying sounds, or to silence.[18] In other words, babies in a hospital nursery tend to cry in empathy for their unhappy counterparts.

But whether empathic distress is indeed instinctive, or rather learned in the early hours of our lives, another person's suffering ignites an emotional response in us.

While psychologists generally agree that empathy ultimately motivates us to help people, they differ in their opinions about why that is. Two names at the center of this ongoing debate are New York University professor Martin Hoffman and University of Kansas professor Daniel Batson.[19]

Hoffman contends that empathic distress triggers a desire to improve another person's well-being, a reaction called *empathic altruism.* Hoffman, whose extensive research on empathy includes observing those crying babies at University of Michigan Hospital, asserts that the link between empathic distress and altruism is intuitive.[20] In other words, witnessing another person's distress causes *us* to become distressed. And our instinctive way of reducing our own distress is to help the other person.

Experts agree that empathy motivates us to help others. But they disagree about the reasons why.

Batson counters that alleviating our distress and helping others are mutually exclusive intentions, and he offers alternatives to Hoffman's explanation of an innate connection between empathy and altruism. While Batson acknowledges that someone else's distress surely causes our own feelings of distress, he points out that our motives for helping that person are as likely to be selfish as altruistic.[21] In other words, we might help someone in order to rid ourselves of our unpleasant empathic distress, as Hoffman suggests. Or we might help in order to avoid social shame or personal guilt for not helping, or to earn the type of social rewards we associate with helping.[22]

Then again, altruism might simply depend on having enough time to help. Batson worked on a study at Princeton University in the 1970s based on the parable of the Good Samaritan, the gospel story of a Jewish traveler beaten by robbers and left for dead on a road. In the parable, a priest and a Levite—both thought to be virtuous men—pass by the injured Jew without helping. Then a Samaritan happens by. Although Jews and Samaritans were said to loathe each other, the Samaritan went to his enemy's aid. In the Princeton experiment, students from the university's Theological Seminary were set up to encounter a clearly distressed "victim," a shabbily dressed actor slumped over and groaning in a doorway. The study's subjects were most likely to ignore the victim when they were in a hurry to reach their destination. Ironically, some of the subjects were asked to present a short talk about the Good Samaritan parable, and they thought they were on their way to perform that task when they hurried past the groaning victim.[23]

Regardless of why some people help others, most would simply rather do nothing.

How do these theories relate to your life? Imagine you're walking down the street when you see a homeless person begging for money. Hoffman's hypothesis is that your concern for that individual's welfare will cause you emotional distress, and that distress will stir you to hand over a few dollars—an instinctive and truly altruistic reaction. On the other hand, Batson's research suggests that while the beggar's heartbreaking appearance might cause you to feel empathy, you could be repulsed instead, or feel nothing at all. Accordingly, your instinct could be to give the person some money, or to absently hurry past on your way to catch a meeting, or to deliberately cross the street to avoid the beggar entirely.

What we can garner from the academic debate about empathy, distress, and why people help is that we all have our own motivations for getting involved with those in need. But while we try to understand what motivates those who help others, it's important to recognize the unavoidable reality that most people tend to do nothing at all. And that leads us back to the question of what inspires people like Joe Works and Mark Stelzner to resist that universal tendency.

Dreading the Thought

When it came time to decide whether he could afford to keep from laying off his idle employees, Joe Works did some calculations. He looked at various scenarios, factoring in how long the recession might last, how far the company's sales might ultimately drop, and how much employee goodwill a layoff would cost him.[24] Works estimated that paying his employees to do community service would strip another 10 percent from B&W's already diminishing bottom line.[25] So why did he do it?

For the same reason that Works agonizes over each hiring decision—making certain there's enough work in the company's pipeline to keep the new employee busy: "Because I dread the thought of laying people off."[26] In other words, Works is trying to avoid the empathic distress that letting workers go would cause him. The distress he associates with downsizing workers probably stems from a personal struggle to make ends meet during another lingering recession.

Joe Works was the middle of five children who grew up farming the land that their great grandfather settled on Humboldt's outskirts in the mid-1800s. Their parents taught them to work hard, to give back to their community, and to plan ahead for farming's inevitable adversities. Fresh out of college in 1971, with dual degrees in Agricultural Mechanization and Business Administration, and with a wife and infant daughter to support, Works set out to find a job. But what he found was a dried-up job market; so he executed his contingency plan and went to work in his family's farming operation.

Despite economists' predictions that the baby boom would continue—and that an ever growing population would create higher food demand and, thus, higher crop prices—the 1970s marked a period of decline for grain farming. The baby boom was finished booming, and so was the farm industry. While many area farmers abandoned Humboldt and moved to larger cities to find jobs, the Works family fought to keep their farm.

A low point for Works came in 1980 while he and his wife Janie were building a new house on the farm. By then they had three children, and Janie was a stay-at-home mom. The couple could not have chosen a worse time to begin constructing a home. That year, in the midst of the Carter recession, the interest rate on their variable-rate construction loan reached 18 percent. What's more, a summer-long, record-breaking heat wave destroyed their corn crop and wiped out the family's income for the year. With their new home far from completion and their fourth child on the way, Janie was forced to find work as a teacher, while Joe took a job welding oil well pumps for a local factory.

"We struggled under the weight of those high interest rates and house payments through much of the 80s," remembers Works.

"There are a lot of lousy ways to treat employees," observes Joe Works.

By 1985, he was welding full time during the day and farming in the evenings and on weekends. It was around that time that he met Roger Baker, a painter at the factory where he worked. Baker had recently built his own truck bed, and the two friends spent their lunch hours discussing how they could turn that prototype into a business venture. They eventually started making flatbeds and trailer hitches in Baker's garage after their factory shifts, and B&W was born.

In the company's early days, its rapidly growing market share offset the temporary setbacks caused by economic recessions. "In 2001," recalls Works, "we were growing market share fast enough that we hardly noticed the slowdown in truck sales." But this downturn is different. As a dominant player in their industry, B&W is feeling the full impact of the Great Recession.

"Farming had somewhat conditioned me to believe that disaster and disappointment were always just around the corner," says Works. But not even the hardships of farming—droughts, floods, or insects—had prepared him for the effects of the Great Recession. "As a business owner, it is terrifying to see that the world we operate in is drastically and rapidly changing."

Now the company's sole owner, Works tries to prevent uncertainty from terrifying his employees. "I learned through my years of doing factory work that there are a lot of lousy ways to treat employees," he says. One way to mistreat workers is to keep them in the dark. "Management needs to provide information about the business to the employees so they feel involved."

Toward that end, Works sets aside time every month to cook for his entire staff. Afterwards, he updates them about the company's financial condition and business prospects before opening the floor to questions. The monthly get-togethers have been a B&W tradition for the past twenty years.

When asked to describe Joe Works in a single word, his friends are likely to answer quiet and unassuming. His wife Janie calls him gentle. His assistant Sally says Works is judicious, which he jokes is too big a word to describe him. Pressed to sum himself up in one word, Works humbly suggests "thoughtful."

However you describe him, Joe Works epitomizes the ripple-out philosophy of Franciscanomics. Whether he's minimizing his own distress by keeping workers busy doing good community deeds, or just naturally altruistic, doesn't much matter to the people of Humboldt. The stacks of thank-you cards and supportive messages he receives never question his motives. They simply voice the town's enormous gratitude for his Francis-like actions.

Earning His Wings

When you first meet Mark Stelzner, you might think that he's trying to sell you something. He has a deep, booming voice that brings to mind a radio announcer pitching a product. But once you listen to him, you'll realize that what he's pedaling is the value of helping others.

On that fateful winter morning in Washington, D.C., while eating his breakfast and struggling to digest the latest unemployment news, Stelzner was struck by the despair the recession was inflicting upon everyone he knew. Now a resident of San Francisco, Stelzner remembers feeling distressed at the thought of millions of unemployed people experiencing increasing hopelessness. "Many of those I met prior to starting JobAngels were suffering in silence," he recalls, "attempting to put on a brave face, but secretly terrified about the severity of the situation."[27]

With the unemployment "wolf" at the door, Americans had reason to be afraid. Business closings were on the rise, as were massive layoffs. In their efforts to shore up the bottom line, even profitable companies had reduced their staffs. One in ten workers was jobless, and hundreds of thousands of additional jobs were disappearing every month. Referring to the workforce's waning sense of job security, Stelzner says, "The historical 'employment contract' that many people took for granted had been, figuratively speaking, burned in the public square. Therefore, even those who remained employed knew that at any moment their positions could be eliminated." His instinct was to find a way to help.

Although the JobAngels movement gained an immediate following, in the beginning, Stelzner realized that most unemployed people felt that they were on their own in dealing with their job loss. Ours is, after all, a nation built through legendary adversity. "As Americans, we're taught to pull ourselves up by our bootstraps and make our own luck," Stelzner points out. "I suspected that we would need to proactively reach out to those in need, as opposed to expecting them to ask us for help."

Hundreds of thousands of jobs were disappearing every month.

As the organization's founder, Stelzner has had a front-row seat from which to watch the recession's impact, and many people and their stories have affected him profoundly. Not long ago, he received a late-evening telephone call from a woman living in a tent city in Arkansas. She had been covering herself with old newspapers to stay warm and, as fate would have it, one of the papers had a story about JobAngels. To Stelzner's dismay, the woman mentioned that she had stolen a cellphone in order to call him for help. Stelzner remembers trying to reconcile his aversion to her criminal act with his empathy for her desperation. He was able to refer her to some nearby nonprofit organizations where she could find help, and then he convinced her to return the phone to its owner.

"I think it's very easy to turn on the news, listen to terrible statistics, and then depersonalize the reality of the situation," says Stelzner, after talking about his interaction with the homeless woman. "JobAngels has humanized and personalized the recession for me. Yet we, as a nation, have so far to go."

Stelzner has also witnessed firsthand how being part of JobAngels has helped the organization's volunteers deal with the emotional aspects of the recession. For many, it has helped them cope with the nagging fear of losing their own jobs; perhaps some believe they're sowing good karma. But volunteers seem mindful that someday they too may need assistance in finding work. In any event, those job angels tell him how being part of the movement has energized them personally.

Especially fascinating to Stelzner is how willing unemployed volunteers are to help other jobseekers. "They share stories, brainstorm solutions, discuss opportunities, and generally lift one another up," he says. His experience with JobAngels has taught Stelzner that, sometimes, people experiencing hardship just need to know that someone cares. "The selfless act of offering a sympathetic ear and listening—truly listening—can make a tremendous difference."

To better equip JobAngels for that supportive role, Stelzner decided to join forces with another grassroots organization in early 2011.[28] The resulting merger between JobAngels and Atlanta-based nonprofit Hiring for Hope (hiringforhope.org) means that jobseekers get networking help and, at the same time, much-needed moral support for dealing with unemployment's devastating effects on their families.

Stelzner says that all it takes to become a job angel is a desire to help. But as he sensed early on, the helper must take the initiative. Perhaps the subjects in the Princeton Good Samaritan study, hurrying to get to their destination, would have been more inclined to assist a scruffily dressed victim if the actor had requested their help. But asking for assistance is not instinctive to most Americans who have been taught to fend for themselves.

So joining the JobAngels movement requires a willingness to take the first step. "One simply needs to pick an individual in need—a friend, a former coworker, a neighbor, a relative, or a complete stranger—and do everything in your power to help that person secure gainful employment."

"From the moment you engage and assist," says Stelzner, "you have earned your wings." *Angel wings,* that is.

A Quiet Movement

All across the country, Americans are finding unique and meaningful ways to deal with the Great Recession.

Some, like those at Boston's Beth Israel Deaconess Medical Center, are helping co-workers keep their jobs. When department heads learned that budget deficits would force the hospital to downsize hundreds of employees, they stepped forward to intervene. Thirteen medical department chiefs volunteered to take annual pay decreases of nearly $27,000 each. The $350,000 in savings was enough to preserve ten staff positions.[29]

But the department heads did not stop there. They sent letters to hundreds of staff doctors and administrators encouraging them to do their part. The response was overwhelming. Physicians and top executives took their own pay cuts, and many made cash donations to the hospital as well. CEO Paul Levy personally matched 10 percent of the initial staff donations. For their part, frontline employees offered to forgo cost-of-living raises, 401(k) matches, and some paid days off. Although Beth Israel ultimately had to let seventy employees go, it was a far cry from the 600 workers that administrators had originally intended to dismiss.[30]

The desire to help others withstand the Great Recession's effects is spreading. Some people are helping co-workers maintain their incomes. Like Clemson University, funding cuts forced the Medical University of South Carolina to impose furloughs on many of its employees. And just like at Clemson, MUSC's staff established a relief fund to reimburse the university's lowest-paid workers for their unpaid leaves. Donations totaled more than $175,000, and benefited approximately half of the 1,200 furloughed workers.[31]

Some people are finding ways to help others while helping themselves. After Seth Reams lost his concierge job in December 2008, he sent résumés to hundreds of potential employers. But the Portland, Oregon, resident didn't get any responses. As his bout of unemployment dragged on, Reams began to feel useless. "I felt like I wasn't a member of society anymore," he says.[32]

That's when Michelle King, Reams' girlfriend, suggested that he do some volunteer work. Recognizing that Reams was not the only laid off person in Portland, the couple soon began conceiving of ways to recruit other out-of-work people to perform volunteer projects in the community. As a result, they started a nonprofit organization called We've Got Time To Help that matches unemployed volunteers with people who need help.

In the first week, Reams tackled the group's maiden project: helping a pregnant woman move into a new home. Since then, more than 100 volunteers have helped with everything from painting rooms in a battered women's shelter to removing overgrown trees. Volunteers include plumbers, roofers, electricians, and gardeners, and these days, the crews include more than out-of-work people looking to stay busy. There are also retirees, small-business owners, and stay-at-home moms volunteering for projects.

But volunteering can involve more than just time. Reams and King have even sold some personal items to raise the money to complete a project for someone in need. And in Reams' opinion, it's worth the sacrifice. "I feel like I'm doing something worthwhile," he says. "It's re-instilled a faith in humanity."

Finally, some people are actively persuading others to help. Philadelphia philanthropist Gene Epstein announced that he would donate $1,000 to charity, every time an area small business hired an unemployed worker. Epstein has pledged to contribute as much as $250,000 in order to encourage business owners to put people to work.[33]

Franciscanomics shows that our collective fate is in our own hands.

These are just a few examples of Franciscanomics in action. They are the stories of caring people who are doing whatever they can think of to save people's jobs and put displaced employees back to work.

Franciscanomics shows that our collective fate is in our own hands. Altruism may or may not be innate, but it can certainly become second nature. We can choose to notice the distressed people we meet as we hurry along the road—those whom the recession has beaten, whose dignity unemployment has stolen—and we can choose to stop and help.

So, in the words of the Mark Stelzner tweet that launched a thousand volunteer job angels, "You game?"

Two

The Foreclosure Activist

On a sweltering summer day in 2009, oncology nurse Lisa Epstein is running down a sidewalk in West Palm Beach, Florida. One of her patients desperately needs help, and Epstein, wearing her nurse's uniform and one of her trademark, brightly colored hair scarves, draws attention as she rushes to the woman's side. Time is running out for the patient, and Epstein only has an hour—her lunch hour, actually—to help her.

You may be thinking that a health complication from her cancer has placed Epstein's patient in peril this day, but that's not the case. In fact, she is afflicted with an economic malady that is plaguing millions of Americans, and it's quite possible that Epstein is the only person who can provide a remedy.

Epstein met Robyn Powell while working at the Palm Beach Cancer Institute. Powell was a patient there, and one day she called her favorite nurse to ask for a different kind of help: she was being evicted from her home and needed the names of some area homeless shelters. Now Epstein was hurrying to support her patient at a final judgment hearing. Powell had planned on skipping the hearing, having already conceded that she was defenseless against the powerful bankers who were repossessing her house. But that changed after she told Epstein her story.

Powell is not the type of person who deliberately shirks paying her debts. Several months before, she was in a Palm Beach hospital recovering from a head-on automobile collision when she suffered an unrelated seizure. Tests revealed that she had a brain tumor. Unable to run her pool-cleaning business while her accident injuries healed and she underwent cancer treatments, Powell got behind in her mortgage payments. Now her mortgage company was foreclosing, and she and her teenage son were about to lose their home.[1]

"The biggest financial crime the world has ever seen," declares Lisa Epstein.

Luckily for Powell, Epstein had recently become somewhat of a foreclosure expert—seeing that she was busy fighting her own eviction notice. She offered to look over Powell's court papers and, despite her lack of formal legal training, noticed that the foreclosure documents neglected to identify what bank actually held the mortgage. So she sat down with Powell and helped her write a letter challenging the foreclosure.

Having convinced Powell to attend her summary judgment hearing, Epstein promised to be there for moral support. Foreclosure judgment proceedings are typically rubber-stamp formalities in which banks submit their cases and overburdened judges decide the fate of hundreds of homeowners in a matter of minutes. After running the several blocks from the Cancer Institute to the courthouse, Epstein now sat beside Powell as she read their letter to the judge.

When the judge learned that the mortgage company's lawyers had failed to show up for the hearing, she granted Powell a continuance. In addition, she contacted the local legal aid office and arranged for a real attorney to represent Powell in the foreclosure. While she carries on her fight against brain cancer, the mortgage company continues to threaten Powell with foreclosure. In the meantime, thanks to Epstein's help, she and her son have been able to remain in their home.[2]

Since then, Epstein has left nursing to become a full-time, self-described "foreclosure activist," helping people like Powell fight back against the predatory lenders who set up millions of homebuyers for failure, and who are now intent on taking away their homes.[3]

To fully appreciate what Epstein is doing to help foreclosure victims endure the Great Recession, you need to understand the background behind the mortgage crisis, or what she fittingly calls "the biggest financial crime the world has ever seen."

The Making of a Housing Bubble

The Great Recession introduced many Americans to the phrase *subprime mortgage.* Bankers use the term when referring to home loans they consider risky because the borrowers have unstable income or unfavorable credit histories. But after the housing bubble burst, and financial institutions were saddled with mounting payment delinquencies, their ensuing actions revealed a hidden meaning in the phrase: lenders had never intended the word "subprime" as a euphemism for a risky *loan,* but as an esoteric, derogatory description of the *people* whose mortgages they pigeonholed into that category.[4]

The crisis began during the 1990s, when mortgage industry regulators relaxed the rules governing home loans. With interest-rate caps removed, banks began charging higher interest rates to low-income borrowers, ostensibly as a way to offset the increased risk of nonpayment these borrowers represented. More significantly, perhaps, deregulation also allowed banks to package their existing mortgages into securities to be sold to investment groups.

Securitization, the practice of selling bundles of mortgages to investors, provided an all-around financial windfall for banks; not only could they rid their balance sheets of fixed-rate mortgages—which, because of their lengthy payment terms, often locked banks into unfavorably low interest rates— securitization also provided an immediate revenue boost. What's more, banks continued to earn ongoing fees for collecting and applying customer payments on home loans long after they sold the notes on the secondary market.

For their part, investors were attracted to the perceived safety of mortgage-backed securities. After all, government-sponsored corporations Fannie Mae and Freddie Mac owned or guaranteed many of the securities. And mortgage-backed securities often provided higher yields than bonds with similar investment ratings. As a result, demand for the securities sky-rocketed.[5]

To feed investor demand for mortgage-backed securities—and to keep the ensuing revenue stream flowing onto their income statements—financial institutions scrambled to find ways to encourage greater numbers of people to buy homes. Toward that end, many banks elected to intentionally increase their exposure to subprime mortgages. Behaving like predators, they lured borrowers with teaser interest rates and monthly payments that were low at first but increased drastically a year or two later. And in their haste to approve mortgages, bank underwriters either neglected to verify applicant income and debt levels, or deliberately ignored information that indicated these borrowers did not have the means to repay their loans.

Bankers claimed to be extending homeownership opportunities to greater numbers of people.

At the same time, banks turned their voracious loan-making sights on low-income and minority borrowers—groups that had long been deprived of bank financing—using high-pressure sales tactics and complicated terms that masked the exorbitant interest costs of subprime mortgages. Consequently, since the mid-1990s, the majority of subprime loans were made in African American, Latino, and low-income communities.[6] Not surprisingly, having been denied access to credit in the past, many predatory lending victims lacked the financial wherewithal to understand the unfair, bank-favoring credit terms they were accepting. For that reason, subprime loans made to minority borrowers are more likely to include costly provisions—such as excessive application fees, large prepayment penalties, and interest-only terms—than similar loans made to non-minority borrowers.

Mortgage bankers justified the pricing inequities by saying that these so-called "risk-based" terms allowed them to fulfill federally mandated obligations to make homeownership available to a larger portion of the population. Higher interest rates and fees were necessary, they argued, to protect their shareholders against the heightened risk that "subprime" customers would default on their mortgages. But, in truth, the higher interest rates they charged on subprime mortgages made the securities that much more attractive to would-be investors. Besides, banks were selling the loans—and passing on their risks—to investors as quickly as they could complete the paperwork.

And, as it turns out, bankers had been hoodwinking investors as well as homebuyers. To ensure their mortgage-backed securities received favorable ratings from credit agencies, financial institutions regularly hid subprime mortgages within bundles of prime loans. Banks also downplayed the amount of subprime debt they held on their balance sheets, thereby deceiving—and jeopardizing—the shareholders they professed to protect.

Leading up to the bubble's rupture, the financial sector's

appetite for subprime mortgages—and the monetary gains that came from securitizing them—had turned many once-respected institutions into predatory lenders. As a result, the subprime mortgage market grew from $35 billion in 1994 to $665 billion in 2005. By the end of 2006, nearly 25 percent of new home loans were subprime mortgages, even though industry experts were warning that one out of five subprime mortgages would end up in foreclosure within two years of being issued.[7]

Why would bankers, whose profession has long been typecast as conservative and overcautious, ignore warnings about foreclosures? Author Tony Schwartz explains that greed is causing some bankers to put short-term profits before common sense. Compensation packages are increasingly dependent on bonuses and stock options—both of which are linked to their companies' financial results—and executives at highflying banks can earn huge payouts. All that money can be addictive, and turn good bankers into predators. "At its most rapacious," writes Schwartz, "greed trumps rationality, judgment, perspective, and any concern with the collateral damage it may cost."[8]

Once the housing market collapsed, financial institutions were forced to write off billions of dollars of subprime mortgages. Then many of those banks attempted to cut their losses by repossessing, and then reselling, the homes of their delinquent customers. And in their rush to cleanse their balance sheets of subprime loans, these companies are employing the same greedy behaviors they used to create the mortgage crisis.

Like predators stalking their prey, bank foreclosure specialists know that speed is essential. People who cannot afford to make their mortgage payments also lack the money to hire attorneys to help them fight foreclosure; armed with that knowledge, financial institutions are overloading the court system with stacks of uncontested filings, and judges have little choice but to issue swift judgments favoring the banks.

Not every predator is as easy to reason with as the wolf of Gubbio proved to be. It requires someone with Saint Francis-like courage to confront the predatory lenders who are largely responsible for the nation's housing bubble, and who are ruthlessly perpetuating its economic aftermath.

Don't Call *Her* a "Deadbeat"

When she applied for a mortgage to purchase her West Palm Beach home, Epstein's credit score was over 800—a nearly flawless rating. With such good credit, she had no reason to suspect that her bank would label her a subprime mortgage customer. Only later, after collectors began foreclosure proceedings against her, did Epstein learn that the lender had classified her mortgage as a *stated income, stated assets* loan. SISA mortgages, as they're called, are loans for which the borrower's declared income and financial resources cannot be verified. That was certainly not true in Epstein's case, but as she would soon determine, it was a very deliberate "mistake."

Flagging Epstein's mortgage as an SISA loan allowed her bankers to structure the loan so that all her payments in the first ten years would be applied to interest only, resulting in higher profits for the bank. Furthermore, given Epstein's strong credit score, tagging her mortgage as "subprime" made it a highly attractive prospect for securitization. But the subprime classification nearly tripled the cost of her private mortgage insurance—a precaution required for borrowers whose down payments are less than 20 percent of the home's value—thereby increasing her monthly payments.

On the day of the closing, Epstein was surprised to learn that her payments would be higher than what her mortgage originator had quoted her. Still unaware that the bank had underhandedly labeled her as a subprime borrower—and, being eight months pregnant, anxious to move into her new home—Epstein agreed to the revised mortgage terms.

Looking back, Epstein acknowledges that trusting her banker—and unwittingly accepting the higher interest rate—was a poor business decision on her part. "I was naïve to believe that banks and borrowers were held to the same laws," she recalls. "I know better now."

She was just one of millions of consumers who assumed that honest and law-abiding leaders were running their banks. These were companies, after all, with renowned names and long histories of financial stability. How could Epstein or any other American be expected to know that the banks portraying themselves as pillars of trust and financial security were actually plotting to exploit them? For Epstein, and others like her, it was a rude awakening.

As a single mother caught up in the Great Recession, Epstein struggled to make ends meet after buying her home, and the unduly high mortgage payments didn't help. Despite her shining credit history, the bank repeatedly denied her requests to modify the mortgage terms. Rather than restructuring the loan to lower her monthly payments when she fell behind, Epstein's creditors chose to foreclose on the home that she shared with her three-year-old daughter.

Unable to afford an attorney, but unwilling to give up her home without a fight, Epstein decided to take on the bank alone. While attempting to educate herself about foreclosures, she stumbled upon her bank's initial ruse, and discovered an industry-wide conspiracy to defraud millions of subprime borrowers, securities investors, and, ultimately, the entire country.

Regardless of the bank name on the documents, the same individual's signature appeared on the forms.

Delving into the paperwork related to her case, Epstein came across three different versions of what were identified as copies of her original note. She also discovered the names of six separate financial institutions on various documents. Incredibly, regardless of which bank's name was listed on the document, the same individual had signed many of the forms, indicating a different job title for each purported employer. As if those abnormalities were not suspicious enough, the document assigning Epstein's mortgage to U.S. Bank—thus giving it authority to foreclose on her home—was dated three months *after* that bank had initiated foreclosure proceedings.[9]

At first, Epstein thought she had uncovered an illicit attempt to repossess her home. "I thought the fraud was on the foreclosure end," she says. But after her persistent research revealed the undisclosed changes to her mortgage, she realized that she'd been deceived all along—that she had been, and continued to be, a victim of predatory lending.[10]

That realization marked a turning point for Epstein. Until then, she'd had a self-centered goal: to hold off the predators who were trying to take her house. But, in true Franciscanomics fashion, Epstein changed her mindset. Rather than dwelling on her own adverse situation, she shifted her focus to helping others.

"Suddenly it went beyond *my* mortgage and *my* foreclosure," recalls Epstein. "It's now about drawing attention to the fraud, and standing up for people who, like me, have been wrongly labeled as 'deadbeats' by big banks."

Since then, she's been educating other foreclosure victims, and waging what she justifiably if not dramatically calls "an essential battle for America to remain a democratic republic."

An Innate Drive

Epstein is not likely to pull any punches when speaking out against predatory lenders, and like any good activist, she has a penchant for sound bites. She refers to subprime loans as "financial weapons of mass destruction," and accuses mortgage lenders of "tearing up the moral fabric of the country." But, sound bites aside, Epstein is helping to alert borrowers, prosecutors, legislators, and fellow activists to the deceit that's prevalent within the home loan industry.

She writes detailed letters to bankers, politicians, lawyers, and Florida Supreme Court justices, drawing their attention to the widespread deceit. She also has a blog called "Foreclosure Hamlet" (www.foreclosurehamlet.org), on which she shares her newfound knowledge and encourages other victims to challenge their foreclosures.

What is it that drives Epstein to take on predatory lenders in a manner reminiscent of Saint Francis confronting a predatory wolf in the Gubbio countryside?

For one thing, she says that her nursing background has sharpened her instinct for helping people in trouble. Without a doubt, through conversations with visitors to her website's chat room, Nurse Epstein draws on her bedside manner to comfort people who are suffering the pain of foreclosure.

"Every American should be concerned," warns Lisa Epstein.

But from a more philosophical perspective, she credits her German-Jewish heritage for providing her the inherent courage to stand up to evil. "In many ways," she explains, "what is occurring in America is no different than what occurred in early Nazi Germany, when a destructive force came into power and marginalized, shamed, and dispossessed a segment of society."

Today, says Epstein, financial institutions are singling out a portion of the population and calling them deadbeats. "Like prisoners in the Nazi concentration camps, who had numbers tattooed on their arms, our identities are being replaced by our credit scores."

Her analogy is a good one. Our country's economic power is in danger of being consolidated by a handful of big banks, run by leaders who have made the giant leap from taking slight advantage of customers to taking extreme advantage of them—to the point where they are oppressing large groups of people.

"Every American should be concerned," warns Epstein, drawing again on the lessons from her heritage. As her German ancestors learned, it's unwise to relinquish power to leaders with evil intentions and expect them to look out for everyone's best interests.

For her part, Epstein won't let a few evil bankers steal her identity, or determine her self-worth. "I'm still the same person I was before they destroyed my credit score," she says.

Who Lisa Epstein is, fortunately for us, is a gutsy and assertive woman who didn't buckle under harsh adversity—a courageous fighter who refused to surrender to the financial criminals who first deceived her, and then tried to bully her into giving up her home. And though the odds remain stacked against her and in favor of the powerful financial behemoths, nothing will stop Epstein from helping others—those caught up in their own legal and emotional battles—fend off predatory lenders.

Collaboration

Through her efforts to help others in their battles to save their homes, Epstein has encountered several likeminded people with the same goal. In Florida, a state hit especially hard by the housing crisis, a small group of extraordinary individuals are making a big difference.

For starters, there's attorney Tom Ice—who Epstein, in a characteristic sound bite, admiringly calls "the Clarence Darrow of the foreclosure crisis." Ice spent much of his legal career practicing corporate law, helping to defend airlines and automakers against accident lawsuits. Then in 2008, with the Great Recession getting worse, he opened his own law office in a Royal Palm Beach strip mall. There, he and his wife Ariane, a paralegal, are helping bankruptcy clients navigate through the foreclosure process.[11]

Not long ago, Ice was representing a Boca Raton woman facing foreclosure by GMAC Mortgage. He remembered reading a seventeenth-century English case study in which a court ruled that borrowers owe their debt to their original lenders, not to bill collectors who subsequently acquire their notes. A 330-year-old ruling buried in English case law has no bearing on a foreclosure proceeding in current-day Florida, of course, but it reminded Ice of how banks had been transferring mortgages through securitization. After a mortgage has been securitized, he wondered, who is entitled to collect the debt?

So, while trying to discern the paper trail in the Boca Raton case, Ice decided to depose Jeffrey Stephan, a GMAC employee whose signature appeared repeatedly on his client's foreclosure documents. During his deposition, Stephan revealed that he routinely signed court affidavits for over 10,000 foreclosures a month, each time falsely attesting to having personal knowledge about the loan's documents. The case earned document processors like Stephan the moniker "robo-signer," and it shed national light on the unscrupulous steps mortgage companies were taking to ramrod foreclosures through the court system.

To keep up with the hundreds of foreclosure cases his firm now handles, Ice has added a staff of lawyers and has had to give up golfing on weekends. But thanks to his resourcefulness, many homeowners, including his Boca Raton client, are able to restructure their loan terms and remain in their homes.

Epstein also praises St. Petersburg consumer-rights attorney Matt Weidner, not only for defending clients facing wrongful foreclosures, but also for being a vocal critic of Florida's "rocket docket" hearings in which judges race through hundreds of foreclosure cases in short order. "Inside these courtrooms," says Weidner, "judges—the bad ones—are just granting summary judgments like nothing's happening. They're abdicating their responsibilities to be real judges."[12]

Another of Epstein's heroes is attorney Lynn Szymoniak, who she applauds for providing *pro bono* legal services to foreclosure clients. Szymoniak is the editor of *Fraud Digest,* an online magazine that publicizes fraudulent schemes in order to build awareness. A former fraud examiner, Szymoniak writes extensively about the foreclosure crisis and appears as an expert defense witness in foreclosure fraud cases.

And last but not least, like his good friend Epstein, Michael Redman is a self-made expert in foreclosures. Redman was helping his fiancée fight eviction when he noticed the identical pattern Epstein and Ice had observed: the same people had signed mortgage assignments for several different banks. "But their signatures never matched," recalls Redman. Obviously, they were not the same people at all.[13]

Redman created a blog called "4closureFraud" (4closure-Fraud.org) where he posts copies of suspicious documents, depositions of loan processing workers, court decisions, and how-to instructions for researching public records. Among those seeking information about foreclosures, Redman says his website has attracted visitors from the Justice Department, the Internal Revenue Service, and the White House.[14]

Epstein is proud to be part of this collaborative group of activists who refuse to wait for government investigators to uncover fraud in the mortgage industry. Through their combined efforts and remarkable initiative, they've been conducting their own inquiries—and the benefits from their findings are rippling out to millions of Americans. Epstein and her cohorts have sounded an alarm that is echoing across the country: the mortgage crisis is not a civil issue; it's a criminal matter. Therefore, deceived borrowers should not have to stand alone, defending themselves against powerful banks in overcrowded civil courtrooms. It's the duty of prosecutors to charge predatory lenders as criminals, and of judges to punish the guilty offenders—not with trivial fines and meaningless reprimands, but with incarceration.

Some authorities have gotten the message. In October 2010, the attorneys general of all fifty states agreed to conduct a joint investigation into mortgage lending practices.[15] To Epstein, the news brought vindication. At last, reporters and prosecutors around the country, who once dismissed her warnings as the ramblings of a deadbeat, were asking the very questions that she had been raising.[16]

A Mother's Wish

Epstein left her job at the Cancer Institution to, as she puts it, "lend the human labor to the divine task of helping people affected by the foreclosure crisis." She's scraping by on her savings right now, and knows that she'll have to return to nursing eventually. What's more, she could not fulfill her activist role were it not for the childcare support of her dear friend, Mary Del Aguila, who she calls her daughter's "second mother." And she acknowledges that the youngster has sacrificed as well, often forgoing mother-daughter time while Epstein prepares for battle against mortgage companies.[17]

But the young girl, who occasionally accompanies Epstein to the courthouse while she conducts research, seems to understand the importance of her mother's work. On one recent trip, Epstein gave her daughter two pennies to toss into a wishing well outside the courthouse. Her first wish was for a bunny; her second wish was that her mom could make judges "understand foreclosures."

When asked what lessons she hopes her daughter will learn from her efforts to help people in foreclosure, Epstein recalls a quote attributed to Albert Einstein: "The world is a dangerous place to live, not because of the people who are evil, but because of the people who don't do anything about it."[18] She hopes her daughter will remember that her mother recognized the evil in the foreclosure crisis and stood up against it.

"Doing good is not always a safe thing to do," says Epstein. "But it's the right thing to do."

Could there be a better sound bite to describe the Franciscanomics philosophy, and the growing numbers of people moved to join in supporting it—whether they realize it or not?

Three

The Stigma Fighters

From the moment Francis heard the figure on the crucifix urge him to "go and repair my church," the future saint began to cherish the symbol of the cross. With its reminder of Christ's painful sacrifice for wayward humanity, seeing a crucifix could literally bring Francis to tears. And though it significantly influenced Francis's early religious life, the crucifix would play an even greater role in his final years.

As summer drew to a close in 1224, Francis and a small group of his followers retreated to a favorite, isolated place on the Italian mountain of La Verna. There, Francis and his companions intended to spend several weeks praying and communing with God. Now in his early forties, Francis was physically exhausted and in failing health—the result of nearly two decades of uninterrupted travel. Forty days of meditation in the peaceful mountainside, he must have thought, would do him a world of good. But a miracle awaited Francis on La Verna—

one that would exact a further toll on his ailing body, and eternally connect him with the cross's symbolism.

While praying alone on the mountain one day, Francis had a vision of an angel hovering above him. As he struggled to fully grasp what he was witnessing, excruciating sores began to materialize on his extremities and side. It was as if nails had pierced his hands and feet, and a lance had punctured his right side. Francis, it turns out, was receiving the Stigmata—a documented phenomenon in which a living person spontaneously suffers wounds resembling those inflicted upon Christ during the Crucifixion.[1]

Stigma: A mark of disgrace; a stain on one's reputation.

Some religious scholars regard the Stigmata as the crowning event of Francis's life—the ultimate culmination of his lifelong quest to identify with and connect to Jesus Christ. To his closest followers at the time, the wounds were physical evidence that God had chosen Francis for the privilege of sharing Christ's earthly experience.

In some ways, the marks left by the Stigmata became an embarrassment—or as the word implies, a *stigma*—to Francis. Contemporary experts speculate that Francis might have wondered if God had punished him—crucified him, no less—for failing the assignment conveyed to him through the crucifix, to "repair" the unrest and strife within His church.[2] That's a plausible explanation for why, in the remaining months of his life,

Francis tried to hide the miraculous wounds from those around him.

Stories like the mystical—and somewhat disturbing—account of the Stigmata are what make Francis a favorite among religious figures. People of just about every faith, and all levels of religious zeal, know Saint Francis as the Patron Saint of Animals and the Environment, and for renouncing his family's wealth, taming the wolf of Gubbio, and receiving the holy Stigmata.[3] Maybe it's the story of the Stigmata that people identify with most. After all, don't we all have wounds to conceal—emotional wounds, that is—lest they be reopened?

Another Kind of Stigma

For more than a decade, Celena Roby carried a stigma of her own. Unlike Francis, the wounds she concealed were not symbols of a divine bond, but the painful markings of domestic violence. At long last, in September 2008, Roby made the gut-wrenching decision to leave her abuser. That she survived the immediate aftermath of that decision could be considered another miracle.

With no work experience and just twelve dollars to her name, Roby had immediate economic obstacles to overcome before she could leave her situation. "I was a stay-at-home mom for those ten years," recalls Roby. "I got involved with my abuser right out of high school. For many years, I would pray and ask God to help me escape, though I was fearful of how I would feed my babies if I did."[4]

Finally, she managed to line up work cleaning houses and doing odd jobs on a construction site, while one of her former teachers with an apartment for rent agreed to let Roby and her sons stay there until she got on her feet. With her prayers seemingly answered, she was ready to escape.

"I was scared and excited at the same time," she remembers. "While I was with my abuser, he controlled every part of my life—when I went to bed and when I could eat. The thought of having that type of independence was indescribable."

Each day, 60,000 Americans flee domestic violence.

On the day he learned that she was leaving him, Roby's abuser became enraged and held her hostage in the bathroom of their West Virginia home. While her two young children pleaded through the locked door for him to stop, he hit Roby repeatedly. "I focused on their cries," she says, referring to her children's pleas, "because I wasn't sure if I'd ever hear that sound again."[5]

After the near-fatal attack was finally over, Roby lay battered with severe head trauma and a serious eye injury. But she was more determined than ever to escape, and she somehow found the strength to take her children and flee to safety.

In making her escape, Roby became one of the tens of thousands of American domestic violence victims who run away from intimate partner abuse every day.

An Ordinary Day in America

For centuries, Francis devotees have observed the miracle that occurred on La Verna as a sacred holiday—the annual Feast of the Stigmata of Saint Francis—on the seventeenth of every September. But in 2008—by pure coincidence, perhaps—September 17 would be a day that underscored the prevalence of domestic violence in America, while serving as a milestone for measuring the Great Recession's effects on intimate partner abuse.

For on that otherwise ordinary Wednesday, the National Network to End Domestic Violence (NNEDV) conducted a twenty-four-hour census of American victims of intimate partner abuse. Throughout the day, the Washington, D.C., advocacy organization collected data from over 1,500 domestic violence programs across the country. The results were staggering: in that one-day timeframe, more than 60,000 adults and children sought refuge from abusive relationships.[6]

In its simplest description, domestic violence is defined as intentional physical abuse that is committed, attempted, or threatened between family members, intimate partners, or cohabitants. More than four out of five cases involve intimate partners, which include current and former spouses, common-law spouses, and boyfriends or girlfriends. Studies in urban areas reveal that 84 percent of intimate partner violence involves a female victim and a male abuser; women abuse men 12 percent of the time; and in 4 percent of all cases, the abuser and victim are the same gender.[7]

Most intimate partner violence occurs in the victim's home, usually in a residence the couple shares. And, as in Roby's case, more than a third of partner abuse incidents take place when children are present.[8]

***

If any problem could benefit from Franciscanomics' ripple-out effect, it's domestic violence.

***

As stunning as the NNEDV figure is, it's important to note that it highlights only the number of people who actually attempted to break free from domestic violence. For an untold number of abuse victims, escape is not an option. Victims face further abuse, or even death, when they try to leave. Indeed, leaving—or making an effort to leave—increases the risk of being murdered by an abuser.[9]

Also disheartening in the NNEDV study is that nearly 5,000 requests for emergency shelter or transitional housing went unmet that day. Many domestic violence programs cannot afford to maintain the staffing levels necessary to meet the growing needs of abuse victims.

The Great Recession, it turns out, has exacerbated domestic violence, while erecting new barriers to fleeing abuse.

The Economy's Impact

Experts have three primary theories about why domestic violence occurs. The *feminist socio-cultural* theory asserts that domestic violence is a consequence of society's historical tolerance of male domination and control over women. The *intergenerational transmission* perspective says that domestic violence is learned at home; in other words, children raised in violent households tend to grow up to be abusive adults. The *psychological* theory claims that individual emotional factors cause violent behavior. Husbands who abuse their wives, for example, show higher evidence of personality disorders, attachment and dependency problems, anger and hostility, and alcohol addiction.[10]

So while recessions alone do not cause domestic violence, economic downturns certainly worsen the problem. Wage freezes, home foreclosures, and other financial insecurities can strain relationships and lead to increased incidents of violence.[11] In fact, partners who are under high levels of financial stress are more than three times as likely to have physically abusive relationships than other couples. Without question, the Great Recession has had an impact: since the NNEDV conducted its census in 2008, 75 percent of domestic violence shelters have seen an increase in the number of women seeking sanctuary from abusive relationships.[12]

High unemployment aggravates the crisis. Men who experience multiple periods of joblessness are nearly three times more likely to abuse their partners than those with steady employment. Some experts blame this tendency on a misconceived need to demonstrate masculinity: unemployed men often feel inadequate in what they perceive as their traditional breadwinner roles, so they may try to compensate by asserting male dominance in other ways—including exerting violence against an intimate partner.[13]

The correlation between economic stress and domestic violence is a reciprocal one. In other words, while unemployment and financial hardships help increase the likelihood of domestic violence, intimate partner abuse often involves the deliberate creation of economic stress. For example, abusers may try to prevent their partners from working, using such tactics as damaging their wardrobes, inflicting visible and embarrassing injuries, prohibiting them from having their own car, and intentionally failing to fulfill childcare responsibilities. This so-called *economic abuse* is aimed at fostering financial dependency and, thus, trapping victims inside violent relationships. Without financial independence, those who do escape face additional dangers: research shows that more than a third of domestic violence survivors become homeless as a result of fleeing an abusive relationship.[14]

Amid the Great Recession, at a time when domestic violence shelters are facing greater need, 84 percent of victim's services providers are experiencing funding cuts.[15] Soaring unemployment, weak retail sales, and falling property values have reduced local, state, and federal tax collections, meaning there's less government money to "trickle down" to social service programs. Many support agencies have been forced to lay off their own workers, resulting in less immediate help for abuse victims in dangerous situations.

If there was ever a problem where the Franciscanomics ripple-out effect was needed, domestic violence is it. And just in time, some remarkable people are stepping forward to help, finding imaginative ways to raise money, increase awareness, help police and prosecutors, and heal the wounds left by domestic violence.

"Celena's Law"

Once she and her children were safe, Celena Roby petitioned for a protection order barring her abuser from contacting her. She hadn't planned on pressing charges against the man. Until, that is, an unnerving question from her youngest son impelled her to file criminal charges.

As it happened, on the night that he held her hostage, Roby's attacker violently demanded that she answer a question. But in his fit of rage, she recalls, he repeatedly insisted that she answer a question he didn't actually ask. "To this day," she says, "I still don't know what the question was."[16]

Nearly a year after the incident, her son asked Roby why she hadn't simply answered the question. "I realized he thought it was okay, that I could have prevented the injuries if I had just done what I was told." Wanting to show her sons that domestic violence is never justified, Roby filed charges against her abuser.

But to her surprise, West Virginia laws lacked a provision prohibiting unlawful restraint. In fact, legal ambiguities in several states permit intimate partner abusers to hold victims against their will. So prosecutors charged Roby's abuser with domestic assault, and then tried to make a case against him for holding hcr hostage. Even though the defendant confessed in court to restraining Roby, the judge's hands were tied, and he declared the man not guilty.

Convinced that legal outcomes like hers discourage battered women from fleeing violent relationships, Roby began campaigning for longer protection orders and speaking out about the ways in which domestic violence cases are prosecuted. She gave awareness-raising speeches to law enforcement groups, nonprofit organizations, and West Virginia lawmakers—each time advocating for tougher measures to protect domestic violence victims. She called and e-mailed legislators about the importance of more stringent laws. But when governmental solutions were not forthcoming, she decided to create one of her own.

Now employed as a concrete worker, Roby was sitting in a dump truck one day, eating her lunch and daydreaming about creating a new law. Envisioning legislation making it a crime to restrain people against their will, she started scribbling her thoughts on some Post-it® Notes she found in the truck's cab. Not long after that, she gathered up her notes and headed off to the West Virginia Coalition Against Domestic Violence, a statewide alliance of domestic violence programs.

"I'm looking to close that loophole," says Celena Roby.

Excited by her ideas, coalition members formed a committee to help her draft a bill to propose to the state legislature. Widely supported by police, prosecutors, and victims' advocates, the bill makes it a first-degree offense to restrain someone using force. West Virginia's governor signed the bill, nick-named "Celena's Law," into law on March 24, 2011.

"I commend Ms. Roby for coming forward and speaking up for all victims of domestic violence as she worked to make this important piece of legislation a reality," said Governor Earl Ray Tomblin.[17]

"A loophole was found to benefit my abuser," says Roby. "I'm looking to close that loophole with this new law."[18]

Sporting the construction look—wearing steel-toed boots and dirt-covered overalls, and with concrete smudged on her face—Roby doesn't resemble a domestic violence survivor. But in much the way that Saint Francis is known for the Stigmata, Roby may be closely associated with the stigma of domestic violence that marked her both physically and emotionally for over ten years. "I believe I endured the bad things that happened to me for a reason," she says. "My trials and scars served to make me the strong and determined person that I've become, so I could help other domestic violence victims."[19]

It's important to emphasize that, like so many whose efforts demonstrate the Franciscanomics mindset, Roby refused to wait for someone else to solve her problems—for a partner to stop abusing her, or for government leaders to introduce broader restrictions on domestic violence. And, while taking matters into her own hands, this brave survivor shifted her focus from her own hardships to helping others and, in the process, became a shining example of how individual efforts can have far-reaching effects that ripple out to countless other people.

One Company's Personal Issue

In addition to trapping their victims with economic control, many abusers impose isolation on their battered partners as a way to keep them from escaping. It's common for abusers to rip home telephones from the walls or confiscate cellphones, thereby preventing victims from reaching out for help. As a result, domestic abuse victims cannot call the police, and some go years without speaking to their family and friends.[20]

To address that problem, Verizon Wireless has come up with an innovative way to provide domestic violence victims with their own cellphones. The program, called HopeLine®, works like this: Verizon encourages people to donate their used wireless phones, most of which the company refurbishes and sells to support the HopeLine program. The rest are given to domestic violence organizations and law enforcement agencies—along with three thousand minutes of free wireless service per phone—to distribute at no charge to abuse victims.

Since beginning the program, Verizon has collected over eight million devices and distributed more than one hundred thousand refurbished phones to domestic violence victims. The company has also donated an excess of 300 million minutes of wireless service so far.[21] Now, recipients of HopeLine phones are able to pass messages to family members, call the police when violence occurs, and work out escape plans with support agencies.

For their part, donors can drop off used cellphones at the company's retail stores, or simply ship them at Verizon's expense. Buyers of new Verizon phones receive a postage-paid shipping envelope with their purchase, and all other donors can download a postage-paid shipping label from the company's website. The company also organizes local cellphone donation drives across the country.

Verizon's commitment to helping victims of domestic violence doesn't end with free phones and complimentary airtime. The company donates millions of dollars to support domestic violence programs nationwide. And by dialing #HOPE from a Verizon Wireless phone, callers are connected free of charge to The National Domestic Violence Hotline, an around-the-clock nonprofit crisis intervention resource with access to over five thousand domestic violence programs and shelters throughout the United States.[22]

What's in it for Verizon? "This is a very personal issue for all of us at Verizon," explains Dan Mean, the company's CEO.

On November 8, 2001, a thirty-three year old Verizon phone store employee named Amy Homan McGee attempted to leave her abusive relationship. Throughout their marriage, her husband abused McGee physically and emotionally, and he regularly harassed her by phone or in person while she was at work. On the day she left him, her parents and two young children waited for her in the car while McGee ran inside to pack a few things. Five minutes later, McGee's husband, who had been hiding in the house, shot and killed her.[23]

Making people aware of domestic violence, then, is a priority for the employees of Verizon. The company's charitable foundation recently provided Penn State University, McGee's alma mater, with funding to produce a PBS documentary about intimate partner abuse. It's called "Telling Amy's Story."

Domestic violence is a widespread crime that threatens the lives of millions of Americans—people of all ages, genders, economic planes, races, religions, or education levels. It is "a very personal issue" that affects us all.

Reading the Signs

When domestic violence ends in homicide, as it did for Verizon's Amy Homan McGee, the victim's loved ones are left wondering what they could have done to prevent the tragic ending. But warning signs that domestic violence will escalate to murder are difficult to spot, even for law enforcement professionals. In fact, in half of all intimate partner homicide cases, police officers had previously responded to domestic violence calls involving the couples and missed the warning signs that a fatal outcome was looming.[24]

Fortunately, a Maryland coalition has developed a groundbreaking program for identifying those domestic violence victims whose situations put them in danger of being murdered or seriously injured by their partners. The Maryland Network Against Domestic Violence (MNADV) created a two-part protocol for law enforcement officers to follow when dealing with domestic violence situations.

Based on research conducted at Johns Hopkins University, MNADV compiled a list of eleven risk-assessment questions—a yes-or-no checklist designed to spot factors that have contributed to domestic violence-related homicides.[25] Police officers on the scene of a domestic assault ask the victim such questions as whether her partner has ever threatened her with a weapon, or whether she thinks her abuser may try to kill her. The probing questions prompt officers to dig deeper into the nature of the abuse, in an effort to uncover indicators that foretell a relationship's potential for ending in homicide.

Only a fraction of future domestic violence murder victims ever seek help.

If the screening suggests that a victim is at high risk, police officers inform her that she is in danger of being killed. That comes as eye-opening news to many victims, especially those for whom domestic violence has long been a way of life. Answering the questions—and, in the process, actually verbalizing their situations—helps victims realize the real peril they face.

The second part of the protocol involves immediately connecting victims with a domestic violence hotline. What the Johns Hopkins research found is that only 4 percent of future domestic violence murder victims ever seek the help of intervention services. Getting victims into the support system greatly reduces their risk of further abuse; in fact, the incidence of re-assault drops by 60 percent when a victim goes to a shelter.[26] So this on-the-spot step involves showing high-risk victims how to find help.

While at the scene of an assault, a police officer telephones a domestic violence hotline and encourages the victim to speak with the intervention specialist on the other end. The support person provides safety-planning information and tries to persuade the victim to go to a shelter. If a victim refuses to talk to the hotline worker—as is often the case—the officer simply relays information between the victim and the specialist.

"We want to give the victim information that will empower her to decide to seek help," explains David Sargent, a retired police officer and current MNADV training consultant. Because it's the victim who has to choose what's best for her, this part of the protocol is all about encouragement. "The police officer encourages the victim to talk on the phone, and the advocate encourages the victim to go in for services."[27]

It's working. In Maryland, 59 percent of victims agree to speak on the phone with a hotline advocate. More importantly, 30 percent avail themselves of counseling or shelter services—a more than seven-fold increase in the 4 percent of high-risk victims that typically seek help. Called the Lethality Assessment Program, or LAP for short, the program is succeeding in connecting abuse victims in lethal situations with services that can keep them alive.

The benefits from LAP, like so many other Franciscanomics-inspiring initiatives, are rippling outward. With MNADV's help, a dozen law enforcement jurisdictions around the country have already implemented the program.[28] But the coalition has loftier goals in mind.

"We want anyone who might come into contact with a victim to know the signs of lethal danger and be able to do virtually the same thing a police officer does—use the screen, say the same kinds of things to the victim, and connect the victim to the local domestic violence intervention provider," says Sargent.[29]

Providing Proof

When someone slashed Tiana Notice's car tires in early February 2009, she felt certain her ex-boyfriend was responsible. Soon after the University of Hartford graduate student had broken up with this man, he began sending her angry notes and harassing e-mail messages. After receiving a threatening text message from him a month before her twenty-fifth birthday, Tiana got a restraining order preventing him from contacting her. Despite a weeks-long pattern of violating the restraining order, police in Plainville, Connecticut, said they could not charge her former boyfriend for damaging her tires without proof.[30]

So her father, Alvin Notice, thought of a way to catch his daughter's abuser in the act. Suspecting that the harasser would vandalize her car again, Notice installed a wireless video camera outside her apartment and pointed its lens toward the area where Tiana parked.

One week after the camera was installed, on Valentine's Day night, the ex-boyfriend did indeed return. But rather than targeting her car, he brutally attacked Tiana. While Notice's camera recorded her screams, Tiana's assailant stabbed her repeatedly. She died before her father could get to the hospital.

Since his daughter's murder, Alvin Notice has been working to help other domestic violence victims identify and prosecute their abusers. Toward that end, he started a nonprofit agency in his home state of Massachusetts that installs video cameras outside of victims' homes. In its first year, the Tiana Angelique Notice Memorial Foundation equipped the homes of seven women, and video from the cameras led to two domestic violence arrests.

"It's worth every bit of my time to see justice for these women," says Alvin Notice.

Notice, a superintendent for the Massachusetts Department of Correction, installs the cameras with the help of an assistant. They fix cameras to all four corners of the house and tie them into a recorder, all of which costs the Foundation around a thousand dollars per home. Notice donates his installation time.[31]

"This makes me feel so good," says Notice. "It's worth every bit of my time to see justice for these women."

The Great Recession is not the best time to start a nonprofit organization, what with people generally curtailing their charitable giving. Nevertheless, the Foundation raises money to buy video equipment through golf outings and a now-annual hockey tournament that pits Notice's Correction department co-workers against each other.[32] Notice hopes to begin raising enough money to expand the program to Connecticut, where Tiana was murdered.

Notice is also an active proponent of tougher domestic violence legislation in Connecticut, including a law that allows judges to require restraining order violators to wear GPS tracking devices that can alert victims when their abusers are nearby.[33]

After losing his daughter to domestic violence—an experience that would leave most fathers consumed by sorrow and anger—Notice decided to channel his grief and anger into helping other potential victims, instead.

Lessons Learned

Embarrassed and confused by the Stigmata, Francis struggled to understand why he'd been chosen to receive the sacred markings. Likewise, victims of domestic violence are embarrassed and confused about the abuse they suffer. But Celena Roby believes that—like He did with Francis—God purposely chose her to carry her stigma.

"We can look back at all the good things that have happened in our lives and, with great ease, say those things happened for a reason," she explains. "It's much harder to examine the bad that has happened and apply that same outlook."[34]

But doing so helps Roby find a silver lining in the years of abuse she endured. "Had I not suffered, I would have had no reason to conceive a new law on Post-it Notes. Now I see why the abuse happened, and what God wanted me to learn from it."

Like job angel, Mark Stelzner, and foreclosure activist, Lisa Epstein, Roby realized early on that her desire to enact change has nothing to do with her own situation. After all, her domestic violence ordeal is over; she has survived and moved to a far safer place, both physically and emotionally. But like Stelzner, Epstein, and everyone else who exhibits the Franciscanomics mindset, Roby found that she personally benefited by helping others.

She has been moved when domestic violence victims—after hearing her speak about tougher laws—tell her how her story has encouraged them in their own struggles with abuse. That's made her journey from victim to lawmaker especially empowering.

"For a long time," Roby says, "I didn't want to face what was happening in my three-bedroom prison. Speaking out about domestic violence made me deal with what I went through and ultimately helped me heal.

"But, for many years I had no voice. Well, I've found it now. And I plan to continue speaking out for those who can't."

Four

The Producer

Twice a week, film producer and philanthropist Peter Samuelson rides his bicycle from his home in the affluent Los Angeles neighborhood of Holmby Hills to the beach at Santa Monica. A few years ago, Samuelson noticed an increasing number of people living on the streets along his favorite bike route. There were so many people, in fact, that he began counting them.

There, surrounded by some of the priciest and most exclusive real estate in the country, sixty-two people were living without a roof, somehow existing outdoors. Samuelson, whose film credits include *Revenge of the Nerds* and *Arlington Road,* made a point of talking to them all—men, women, and children—to understand their plight. Asking one woman where she slept at night, she pointed to an empty refrigerator box— her improvised refuge. The grotesque disparity between the woman's living situation and his own struck a nerve with Samuelson. "I had to do something about the lady living in a refrigerator box near where I sleep in a house with a refrigerator," recalls Samuelson.[1]

Samuelson, who grew up in London and moved to Los Angeles in 1975, was intent on finding his homeless neighbors an alternative to cardboard shelters. Envisioning a multipurpose, mobile invention that would provide storage during the day and protection and privacy at night, he sponsored a contest at the Pasadena Art Center College of Design, asking participants to develop his basic idea. The winning concept featured a foldout, canvas-covered platform that keeps its sleeping occupant off the ground. Several prototypes later, the street-ready version was a portable individual shelter that the *Los Angeles Times* described as "a cross between a shopping cart and a pop-up camper."[2]

"I had to do something," recalls Peter Samuelson.

Each unit has bins to hold recyclable items—a primary income source for those living on the street. There are brakes to keep the shelter from rolling when parked, and locks to secure personal belongings stored inside. The cover is made out of flame-resistant, military-grade canvas that's strong enough to withstand heavy rain and wind.

Samuelson named his portable home the EDAR (pronounced ee-dar), which stands for "Everyone Deserves A Roof." Next, in the middle of the Great Recession, he started a foundation to raise money for EDARs and distribute them free of charge through homeless shelters and other social service providers. Samuelson's foundation, also called EDAR, built and issued close to 200 units in its first two years. It costs less than $500 to make an EDAR, with donated supplies and labor helping to keep expenses low.[3] Most of the funding comes from Samuelson and small contributions made through the organization's website (EDAR.org).

Finding creative ways to help people who are struggling is something Samuelson considers everyone's obligation. "It's not morally acceptable to let people remain in miserable circumstances, if you aren't offering alternatives," he says.

Nevertheless, there are some who question whether the EDAR represents a sensible approach to dealing with homelessness. Do people living on the street need a better makeshift shelter, or do they need a permanent solution? Are initiatives like these, regardless of how well intentioned their conceivers may be, actually regressive in nature?

Such questions are part of an ongoing national debate about homelessness. The answers are, of course, a matter of opinion. But whatever their opinion is, the Great Recession *has* changed the way many people are tackling social issues.

And, when it comes to homelessness, the outcome may surprise you.

The Scope of the Homelessness Problem

As Peter Samuelson demonstrated, accurately counting the homeless within a high-priced suburb of Los Angeles is a fairly easy task. However, considering the transient aspect of homelessness, determining the actual number of people without a permanent place to live on a national scale is nearly impossible. That said, estimates by government agencies and homeless advocacy groups offer a shocking snapshot of the problem in the United States: in the course of a typical year, over three million Americans experience homelessness.[4]

The numbers are even more overwhelming when examined from a daily basis, as the U.S. Department of Housing and Urban Development (HUD) did in June 2011. From point-in-time data the agency collected on a late-January night in 2010, HUD determined that there are nearly 650,000 homeless people in the country on any given day. And more than a third of those homeless people are *unsheltered,* meaning they are living in doorways, abandoned buildings, cars, parks, train or subway stations, or, as HUD phrased it, other places "not meant for human habitation."[5]

Families comprise a third of the U.S. homeless population.

The good news is that the number of homeless *individuals* has been dropping in recent years, in large part because of successful initiatives to reduce chronic homelessness among those affected by mental illness and substance abuse. But, at the same time, the number of homeless *families* continues to rise. HUD's data showed a 35 percent increase in the number of sheltered homeless families since 2007, with families now comprising a third of the homeless population.

We can blame the Great Recession for the increase in homelessness among families. Unemployment—the clenching jaws of the recession's savage "beast"—is the leading cause of family homelessness.[6] But it may surprise you to know that 19 percent of homeless adults actually have jobs. Indeed, the Great Recession's repercussions are making it tougher for many Americans—even those fortunate enough to have jobs—to afford housing.

Here's why. For a good number of American workers, incomes have remained flat or actually fallen during the Great Recession. Many employers, attempting to remain profitable—or at least minimize their losses—have frozen or reduced wages, eliminated overtime, imposed furloughs, and forced employees to pay a greater share of their health care premiums. Downsized workers, when they're able to secure new jobs, are finding that employers are generally paying lower wages.[7] Meanwhile, housing costs are rising. The net effect of all this is that more and more Americans are using a larger portion of their take-home pay to keep a roof over their heads.

Which is putting them in economic peril. Keep in mind that financial advisors usually recommend budgeting a maximum of 30 percent of after-tax income on housing expenses, including mortgage payments or rent, utilities, and upkeep. Spending more on housing means sacrificing on other necessities such as food, transportation, insurance, and medicine. But with their incomes stagnant or falling, more than forty million households now spend over a third of their income on housing. Alarmingly, housing costs consume more than half the income of the nearly one in five households that make up the workforce's lowest earners.[8]

Considering the foreclosure crisis, it's easy to regard homelessness as a problem that primarily affects homeowners. To be sure, foreclosure-based evictions are contributing to the increase in family homelessness. However, the high housing-cost-to-income ratio is especially widespread among renters who, in general, have much lower incomes than homeowners do.

Facing the greatest housing-cost burden, perhaps, are the 4.5 million single parents—and their nine million children—whose incomes fall in the bottom quartile. Fully half of these households spend at least 64 percent of their incomes on housing.[9] Inevitably, many of these families are forced to choose between having a permanent place to live and covering other life-sustaining expenses.

Undeniably, the homelessness problem is getting worse. Cities all across the United States reported a 9 percent increase in the number of families experiencing homelessness in 2010. One in 200 Americans spent a night in a homeless shelter at some point during the year. To make matters worse, overcrowded shelters turned away 27 percent of the people who came seeking a place to stay.[10]

With its devastating effects on employment and the simultaneous erosion of worker's wages, the Great Recession is spawning poverty throughout our country, forcing greater numbers of people into the bottom layers of the socioeconomic hierarchy. At a time when the gap in wealth between rich and poor Americans is growing wider, the number of our nation's have-nots is getting bigger. Not surprisingly, an increasing number of Americans are just one missed paycheck, a prolonged illness, or an incapacitating accident away from becoming homeless.

One More Stigma

Author Jason Adam Wasserman likes talking about the time he accompanied his mother to a local soup kitchen when he was ten years old. Wanting him to feel grateful for his family's good fortunes, Mrs. Wasserman took her son along to help feed needy individuals who had nowhere else to turn. On their way back home, his mother asked him how he thought the people in the food line became homeless. After reflecting for a moment on something he'd heard his grandfather moralize about—the importance of individual financial responsibility—the youngster surmised, "Bad investments."[11]

Now a college professor and sociologist, Wasserman has a better understanding of what causes homelessness. Over the course of four years, he and fellow researcher Jeffrey Michael Clair immersed themselves in the homeless culture of Birmingham, Alabama, by sleeping under bridges, eating in shelters, and staying in urban camps. They interviewed the homeless individuals they met to determine why so many preferred living on the streets to staying in shelters. Their research, documented in their book, *At Home on the Street*, sheds light on the common misconceptions about homelessness—and the broad difference in perceptions between those who have homes and those who don't.

In a sense, Wasserman's childhood "bad investment" theory was similar in nature to the reasons many people offer to explain homelessness today. For the most part, we choose to believe the stereotypes that portray all homeless people as financially careless, lazy, mentally ill, or addicted to drugs or alcohol. It's somehow reassuring to assume that homelessness is self-inflicted, or even an individual decision. After all, the alternative explanation—that homelessness is something that happens *to* people, and that uncontrollable circumstances could plunge any of us into homelessness—are much too frightening to accept.

> # We choose to assume that homelessness is self-inflicted, rather than something that happens *to* people.

So rather than seeing homelessness as an economic condition, we prefer to make it a social stigma—to view the homeless as people who deliberately deviate from society's norms. As if to validate that notion, we point to those street dwellers who decline to avail themselves of the shelters and social service programs intended to help them. And as Wasserman and Clair discovered, by allowing this stigmatized view to influence our approach to dealing with homelessness, we have made many of our supportive services unappealing to the people who need them most.[12]

For example, the authors found that most homelessness programs are geared toward individuals with drug addictions or mental illness. On the other hand, only a handful of programs address the needs of those made homeless by economic misfortune, such as losing a job or being stuck in a minimum-wage career. And those shelters that do offer help finding work or learning new skills often make job-related training contingent on enrolling in substance-abuse treatment.[13]

"It seemed the shelters dealt with addiction and mental illness almost exclusively," recalls Wasserman. "That's great if that's your problem, but alienating if it's not."[14]

All this has led to a discouraging spiral of despair. Social service organizations persist in offering disaffecting solutions to homelessness, while wondering why countless needy individuals refuse their help. Homeless people, believing that supportive service providers are disconnected from their needs, reject traditional programs and develop an overall distrust of social workers. The majority of the public, distressed by the growing homelessness problem—but seemingly content to wait for an institutional answer to trickle down to the streets—has lost faith in the authorities they've entrusted with the task of finding a solution. Everyone knows more needs to be done; but no one knows where to start.

Or, for that matter, who will take the lead in getting things started.

A Modest Difference

Peter Samuelson never believed for a moment that the EDAR—the combination shopping cart and personal camper that he created—would singlehandedly solve the homelessness problem in America. He simply set out to improve the daily lives of people living on the streets—to make their journeys out of homelessness a bit more bearable in the short term.

But first he had to deal with disparaging questions from EDAR's critics, some of whom accused Samuelson of perpetuating homelessness by enabling people to live on the streets. Along those lines, one city's mayor called the EDAR "regressive" and refused to allow the units in his community.[15]

"Why is the EDAR not regressive? Because it is not nearly as good as a shelter bed," explains Samuelson in his lingering British accent. "There's no pretense it's as good as permanent or temporary brick-and-mortar housing."[16]

> ## "This is a modest way to make a difference in people's lives," says Peter Samuelson.

That's why, when Samuelson first decided to get involved with homelessness, his initial thought was to build more shelters. But Los Angeles, a city with twice the national per-capita rate of homelessness, would need 35,000 additional beds to accommodate its unsheltered homeless population. And at a cost of up to $100,000 per bed to build, Samuelson quickly realized that constructing the shelter capacity necessary to house all of his city's homeless would cost billions of dollars. So, in the EDAR, he found another, more immediate way to help.

"This isn't a distraction from the long-term goals," says Samuelson. "This is a modest way to make a difference in people's lives." And that difference, he points out, is "a lot better than a damp box on a rainy night."[17]

Samuelson happily reports that he hears little opposition these days. "It has become quite clear that EDAR works well and has great value," he says. Still, he has an invitation for the rare detractor ignorant enough to suggest that homelessness is largely self-inflicted—or a personal lifestyle choice.

"Come down to San Julian Street with me," he offers, referring to the heart of L.A.'s Skid Row. "Explain that pompous argument to the hundreds of single women, to the children, to the old ladies shivering to death, to the men who have been sober for a decade, to those who have had jobs for thirty years who have been made homeless by the recession."

Samuelson faults those corrupted banks, insurance companies, and Wall Street firms whose unethical behaviors fueled the current economic crisis for adding to the Skid Row population.

"These are the people on the pointy end of those companies' mistakes," he points out. "Many are not chronically homeless. They fell into homelessness when their employment faded away with the recession. And virtually every single one of them wants nothing more than to have a place to live."[18]

Breaking the Spiral of Despair

After producing an initial run of sixty units, Samuelson imagined himself loading up a truck and driving around Los Angeles, handing out EDARs to homeless people he met. He knew, however, that without a long-term plan for moving people out of homelessness and into permanent housing, the EDAR would prove to be little more than a band-aid initiative. So his foundation began partnering with area churches and homeless shelters to distribute the units.[19]

Today, those supportive service providers are finding that offering EDARs is an effective first step in steering homeless individuals toward permanent housing. Giving away EDARs allows social workers to initiate dialogue with the so-called "shelter resistant" homeless—and gradually earn their confidence. Over time, EDAR recipients begin visiting shelters for food, bathing, or counseling, before finally transitioning into long-term housing programs.

Some shelters even go so far as to let EDAR owners bring their units indoors overnight, a strategy that helps overcome two common obstacles to getting people off the street. First, EDARs allow facilities with limited numbers of beds to accommodate more people. Second, the EDAR addresses the lack of privacy in shelters—a primary reason why many homeless people are reluctant to sleep in shelters.

Whether helping social workers establish critical relationships with homeless people, or increasing the number of people shelters can house, EDARs are helping to break the spiral of despair. Thanks to Samuelson, social service agencies have a new way to connect with people who ordinarily decline their assistance. EDAR recipients are seeing social workers—and their ability to provide practical solutions—in a new light, an important first step in getting them to accept help escaping from homelessness. As a result, Americans are witnessing how one person's actions can help ease the pain of homelessness, even in a modest way.

And that's the start we've been looking for.

100,000 Homes

As researchers Jason Adam Wasserman and Jeffrey Michael Clair found during their interviews of the homeless in Birmingham, Alabama, most supportive service agencies have it all wrong when it comes to solving chronic homelessness. The typical strategy is to begin by offering programs aimed at treating drug addiction and mental illness—which are, unarguably, the leading causes of persistent homelessness. However, the trouble with this approach is that homeless people are not considered "housing ready" until their other problems are behind them, and that prolongs their homelessness. But since 1992, one organization has had great success in reversing the order of events.

> # The goal is to get people off the streets, while improving their chances of *staying* off the streets.

Bucking the status quo was the idea of New York City psychologist Sam Tsemberis. While he was treating homeless individuals for psychological and substance abuse problems, Tsemberis witnessed the spiral of despair firsthand. His patients often went from the streets to emergency rooms, shelters, or jail cells, only to return to the streets. When he asked them what they wanted first, they would consistently answer, "A place to live."[20]

So Tsemberis started an organization called Pathways to Housing, and its cornerstone program is a process known as Housing First. In contrast to the traditional homeless programs Tsemberis had seen in New York, Housing First begins by helping homeless people secure permanent housing, and *then* follows up with the supportive treatment services they need. With their housing situations stabilized, clients are better equipped to tackle issues like drug abuse, mental illness, unemployment, and lack of education. The approach not only gets chronically homeless people off the streets, but it also improves their chances of *staying* off the streets.

Nearly two decades later, supportive housing developer Common Ground decided to put the Housing First model to the ultimate test. In July 2010, the New York-based nonprofit launched a three-year, nationwide campaign to find permanent housing for 100,000 chronically homeless Americans. The ambitious 100,000 Homes Campaign revolves around teaching communities across the country how to use Tsemberis's system to move people out of homelessness and into permanent housing.[21]

Eighty-six communities joined the campaign in its first year, and over 10,300 people were housed.[22] The campaign has its own website called 100,000 Homes (100khomes.org) with real-time placement results, and information about the ways that communities can join the movement.

Rosanne Haggerty, Common Ground's founder, sees one

benefit from the adversity caused by the Great Recession. While the downturn has exacerbated the homelessness problem, it has also inspired thousands of volunteers to embrace the 100,000 Homes Campaign.

"We're all feeling so concerned for our neighbors who are struggling now," says Haggerty. "This is a way to do something…and I think the feeling of having the power to change things is something that many people are looking for these days."[23]

A Single Candle

Peter Samuelson describes himself as a "serial social entrepreneur."[24] It's a fitting label, actually, considering his propensity for getting involved. In 1982, Samuelson established Starlight Children's Foundation to brighten the lives of children with life-threatening illnesses. The international nonprofit organization helps children cope with the challenges of prolonged ailments by educating them about their diseases and fulfilling their special wishes. Then, in 1999, Samuelson founded another organization—First Star Inc.—a national charity that advocates on the behalf of abused and neglected children.[25]

The movie industry, Samuelson believes, has helped prepare him for his role as a social entrepreneur.

"My experience as a film producer has given me the skills and mindset to continue pursuing goals in the face of repeated failure," he acknowledges. "It has provided me with the ability to sell goals that others cannot see—to conceptualize things that do not yet exist, and then to drive them to happen."[26]

So what motivates Samuelson to produce ways of helping people deal with their hardships? Is it the need to alleviate empathic distress—the emotional anguish that psychologists attribute to witnessing someone else's suffering? Or is he a Good Samaritan who—in contrast to the majority of people who would simply pedal past the homeless they encounter, and choose a different bike route the next time—is drawn to those who need help?

For Samuelson, it's simply a matter of equality. It's about parents of healthy children providing emotional support to families of seriously ill kids. It's about grownups standing up for mistreated and forgotten children. And it's about individuals who are lucky enough to have houses and refrigerators helping people whose makeshift homes are the discarded cardboard boxes those appliances came in.

"I am offended by unfairness," says Samuelson. "It drives me crazy."

Crazy like Saint Francis, perhaps, whose good sense many questioned, but whose compassion fueled his devotion to doing good deeds.

You might be wondering what became of the woman whose refrigerator-box-turned-shelter inspired the EDAR's invention. "One of the big issues with our homeless clients is that they are devoid of any permanent addresses, cellphones, or any other ways to keep in touch with them," says Samuelson. "Regrettably, I could never find her after that."

Although Samuelson knows that he's merely scratching the surface of the homelessness problem, like others who exhibit the Franciscanomics mindset, he's never content to sit by and do nothing. "It's better to light one candle than to curse the darkness," he reasons, quoting the Chinese proverb.[27]

It's intriguing that Samuelson would choose that phrase, seeing how an earlier "social entrepreneur" once used similar words to exemplify how a problem's monumental size will not stop a determined person from making a difference. "All the darkness in the world cannot extinguish the light of a single candle," this do-gooder said.[28]

His name? Saint Francis of Assisi.

Five

The Hunger Heroes

Do you know what it means to be hungry? By that, I'm not asking if you've ever experienced the kind of economic hardship that prevented you from having enough to eat. I mean, quite literally, do you know what the word *hunger* means?

A group called the Committee on National Statistics worries that you might be confused by the word. Part of the National Research Council, CNSTAT's job is to improve the reliability of the statistical data government officials depend upon when establishing U.S. policies.[1] Because the federal government keeps track of hunger—and, importantly, how well its taxpayer-supported assistance programs are addressing the problem—officials need valid data.

But if Americans don't actually understand what hunger is, they might provide inaccurate information to researchers, thereby skewing the data. That logic led CNSTAT to recommend that the U.S. Department of Agriculture limit the number of references to *hunger* in its annual assessment of—you guessed it—hunger.

The USDA has been measuring household "food security" nationwide since 1995. Until a few years ago, it classified households without adequate food as either "food insecure without hunger" or "food insecure with hunger." The USDA's definition of *hunger* is the "uneasy or painful sensation caused by a lack of food" brought on by not having enough money or other resources to acquire said food. For a decade, those classifications were used to illustrate that hunger was indeed a growing national health crisis.[2]

But critics charged that the USDA's research findings were overstating the problem. *Hunger,* they argued, is a politically charged word that brings to mind crop failures, famines, and, worst of all, *government inefficiency.* Using the word in research is deceptive, they further reasoned, because the general public is incapable of distinguishing between starvation and simply not having consistent access to food.[3] And if the USDA data is misleading, well then, maybe hunger isn't a real crisis after all.

The USDA eliminated the word *hunger* from its research on hunger.

The USDA responded to that criticism in 2006 by asking CNSTAT to review its survey methods. As if to ensure public confusion, the committee suggested that the USDA use the word *hunger* only when referring to "a potential consequence of food insecurity that, because of prolonged involuntary lack of food, results in discomfort, illness, weakness, or pain that goes beyond the usual uneasy sensation."[4]

That fall, the USDA announced that it would change its classifications to "food insecure" and "very low food security." In other words, the agency was purging the word *hunger* from all surveys and reports discussing hunger.

The criticism, of course, did not end there. Anti-hunger advocates joined the discussion, accusing the USDA of sugar-coating the severity of hunger in America for political purposes. Politicians contending that hunger wasn't a problem worthy of government intervention—since it's nothing more than an "uneasy sensation"—had won their argument simply by ending all use of the "h" word.

If this political maneuvering seems far-fetched to you, if you have a hard time imagining elected officials intentionally manipulating our national vocabulary for political reasons, consider offshore oil drilling and reducing taxes, two recent topics of public debate. These are issues that political pollster and consultant Frank Luntz touches on in his book, *Words That Work,* when he dissects the political capital gained by selecting the right turns of phrase. Luntz points out that the expression *drilling for oil* elicits mental images of "liquid black goo gushing into the sky," followed by the potential for environmental disaster. That's why he encourages pro-drilling politicos to use the less off-putting term *exploring for energy,* instead.

As for cutting taxes, when opponents condemn politicians for proposing an elimination of the *estate tax*—which sounds, accurately enough, like a tariff that affects only wealthy Americans—he advises lawmakers to substitute the all-encompassing and inflammatory name *death tax*. "These changes may not seem significant on the surface," writes Luntz, "but they have had considerable impact on public opinion."[5]

Important point. Because, if there's anything politicians care about, it's public opinion.

George McGovern, the former U.S. senator and presidential candidate who devoted much of his life's work to combating hunger, said that by admitting the existence of hunger in America, politicians would have to "confess that we have failed in meeting the most sensitive and painful of human needs," and such an acknowledgement might "cast doubt on the efficacy of our whole system."[6]

So is dropping the word *hunger* a sincere effort to tweak the reliability of scientific research? Or is it really an attempt to brush an embarrassing national issue under the political carpet?

To be sure, *hunger* conjures up images of harsh despair, and could evoke empathic distress—the psychological anguish we feel in response to other people's suffering. But *food insecurity,* with its euphemistic vagueness, makes the whole issue seem less critical and, thus, easier to ignore.[7]

Whatever the reason for eliminating the word *hunger* from both research and political discourse, the underlying statistics bear out this fact: Too many people are going hungry in our country. And the Great Recession has increased those numbers even more.

The Numbers on Hunger

In the eight years from 2000 through 2007, the percentage of U.S. households without enough to eat was shocking but consistent: in each of those years, between 10 and 12 percent of the country's families were "food insecure," meaning there were times when they could not adequately feed every member of their households. Nearly a third of those households faced episodes of *very low* food security—periods when some family members experienced the physical side effects of going without food. Although food insecurity is mostly temporary—an unforeseen outlay depletes the family's cash, for example—the condition was a chronic problem for a third of those households experiencing very low food security.[8]

By 2010, one in six Americans was food insecure.

Then, in 2008, the first full year of the Great Recession, the percentage of food-insecure households jumped to 14.6 percent. More than seventeen million households were food insecure, while almost seven million households had very low food security. As the Great Recession took hold, the number of hungry families grew to its highest point since the USDA began measuring food security in 1995. By 2010, more than

50 million Americans were living in food-insecure homes, a 39 percent increase since the Great Recession began in December 2007. One in six Americans was food insecure, including a quarter of the country's children.[9]

Without question, the Great Recession had a major impact on food insecurity and hunger. Predatory lending victims saw their mortgage interest rates increase, along with their monthly payments. Energy prices soared, forcing people to pay more to fill their gas tanks. And a tenth of the country's population was out of work, often for extended periods of time. The downturn's effects on household incomes forced a growing number of people to choose between buying food and fueling their cars, or heating their homes, or filling their drug prescriptions. At the same time, participation in the federal Supplemental Nutrition Assistance Program—formerly known as the Food Stamp Program—increased from twenty-five million Americans to 33.5 million.[10]

While economic experts were announcing that the Great Recession was over, its effects on hunger lingered. Months after the recession's official end date, Feeding America's Vicki Escarra shared sobering news from the charity's frontlines: "Our network food banks are calling us every day, telling us that demand for emergency food is higher than it has ever been in our history."[11]

"An Angel" in Queens

As darkness falls each night, a group of hungry men begins to gather on the corner of Roosevelt Avenue and Seventy-Third

Street in Jackson Heights, Queens. Above them runs the elevated Number 7 train—New York's "Flushing Local" subway line—that transports the neighborhood's residents to Midtown Manhattan and back. The community's light and airy apartment buildings, surrounded by their celebrated private gardens, attracts commuting professionals who can't quite afford Manhattan rents. But the men who congregate under the elevated train's tracks don't have offices in Midtown; they are day laborers, and they stand on that same corner every morning waiting for building contractors, farmers, or manufacturers to drive by and hire them for a shift.

The Great Recession has dried up the work, and the laborers often wait for days to no avail. Not surprisingly, many of the men are homeless and most of them are hungry. It's the hunger that brings them to Roosevelt and Seventy-Third at night.

For, every evening around 9:30, Jorge Muñoz arrives at the corner in his pickup truck, its bed full of home-cooked food for the men.[12] *Every* night.

As the men eagerly wait in line, Muñoz passes out Styrofoam containers filled with hot food, coffee, and hot chocolate, all prepared with the help of his mother and sister in the tiny kitchen of the house they share in nearby Woodhaven. For most of these men, it's the only meal they will eat all day.

Muñoz is not a social worker, and his efforts are not part of a government-sponsored initiative. He's just an ordinary person determined to feed some hungry people. With the exception of some donated food, he pays the expenses for this homemade operation out of the modest salary he earns as a school bus driver.

"Every single night, Jorge is here," a grateful recipient of his generosity told a *New York Times* reporter. "He's an angel."[13]

Muñoz first noticed the day laborers gathering under the subway tracks in the summer of 2004. Stopping at the intersection to talk with them, he learned that many were undocumented immigrants desperate to earn money to send back home to their dependent relatives. With work scarce, most were scrimping any way they could to send something home, even if that meant going without food themselves.

Muñoz had to help. Friends who worked for a local food company had mentioned to him that their employer often threw out large amounts of leftover food. Soon after that, while picking up summer school students on Long Island, he watched from his bus as workers dumped food into trash containers behind an airline meal packaging plant. He began thinking of ways to put all those discarded leftovers to good use.

"One day Jorge just came in and asked for extra food for his guys," recounts one of the business owners. Eventually, a few of the companies he approached agreed to donate food that would otherwise go to waste.

Muñoz started small, providing simple brown bag meals to eight workers a few nights a week. Word spread quickly, and the assembly of hungry workers under the train tracks grew. To meet the increasing demand, he recruited his mother, Doris Zapata, to cook, and before long they were providing dozens of free hot meals every night.

Now there's no turning back from his commitment to "his guys." Muñoz established a nonprofit organization called "An Angel in Queens," a name that reflects the headline of a local news story about him. In the wake of the Great Recession, with a greater-than-ever need, he now provides as many as 150 meals a night. A few friends and a young nephew have begun helping out in the kitchen, and his sister, Luz, often accompanies him on the deliveries. A handful of local restaurants and bakeries give him what food they can, and he receives small cash donations through the organization's website (anangelinqueens.org).

"They just wait for me. And I say, 'Okay, no problem,'" says Jorge Muñoz.

The work is exhausting. Muñoz starts his weekdays before sunrise, heading off to drive his school bus. After a full day's work, he comes home around 5:00 to help prepare the evening's meals. On a typical day recently, Muñoz and his helpers cooked fifteen pounds of pasta, twenty-two pounds of rice, sixty pounds of chicken, and ten pounds each of frozen vegetables, onions, and peppers. The menu changes daily, depending on the amounts and types of donations he receives.

The pickup truck is loaded by 8:30, leaving Muñoz just enough time to stop off at church before heading to his corner by 9:30. So far, he's only missed one night, when a heavy snowstorm kept him off the roads. By his count, he has served more than 120,000 meals.[14]

Muñoz never wonders whether his ravenous beneficiaries have *low* or *very low* food security. Nor does he ever ask them their take on the word *hunger*. He leaves the semantics to politicians. He just feeds everyone he can.

"These guys, they got nothing," he says, referring to their lack of food and housing—and the fact that, for many of them, their loved ones are far away.[15]

"They just wait for me. And I say, 'Okay, no problem.'"

"Columbia"

Still, you might ask, why does Muñoz take personal responsibility for these immigrants?

Queens, like all of New York, is known for it's rich cultural diversity. Nearly half of Queens County's two million inhabitants were born outside the United States.[16] That diversity is evident among the workers whom Muñoz feeds. Most of them come from Latin America, Asia, or Europe. And, rather than using their given names, these immigrants respectfully call each other by the countries of their birth. Accordingly, the men have dubbed Muñoz "Columbia."

Muñoz emigrated from Columbia in the mid-1980s. His father died in an accident when Jorge was nine years old, leaving his mother to raise him and his sister alone. Once her children were grown, Doris Zapata came to the United States to work as a live-in nanny for a Brooklyn family. Jorge and Luz followed, two years later.

"We were immigrants and we were illegal," Zapata says, recalling her fear of being found out by police or immigration officers.[17] They obtained legal residency in 1987, and all three are now U.S. citizens. But their frightening experiences as illegal residents are what motivate Muñoz to help the laborers in Queens.

"It's like seeing me, twenty-something years ago, when I came to this country," explains Muñoz of the connection he feels with the homeless, hungry men.[18]

The stories he hears on the corner are heartbreaking. A man once hired three of the laborers to work on his upstate New York farm for several weeks and paid them with a single check. None of the men had a bank account, so they asked Muñoz to cash the check for them. "The check was no good," he recalls, adding that it's common for day laborers to be bilked of their pay. Workers often toil all week with the promise of being paid on Friday; but when payday comes along, the employer is nowhere to be found.[19]

Those are stories of modern-day feudalism—tales of faceless bosses who send their deputies to retrieve immigrant peasants from street corners, extract labor from them, and then cheat them of their wages. But rather than expressing outrage, most Americans seem willing to overlook such grave mistreatment of undocumented workers who are, after all, in the country illegally. It's as if our personal hardships amid the Great Recession have numbed us to the heartless abuse of others—especially when that abuse is inflicted upon those so desperate for the opportunities America promises, they'll do whatever it takes to get here. To Muñoz's guys, it must seem that America has broken its promise.

That's why he steadfastly works to make certain the immigrants have something—a hot meal, at least—on which they can depend. When he's not driving his bus, virtually all of his free time is spent working to feed the laborers. His house is packed wall-to-wall with provisions. One half of the dining room holds a large freezer, and the other half is stacked with crates of fresh food. The living room is lined with boxes of canned goods, bags of dried pasta, and supplies of plastic and Styrofoam containers. Condiments are stored outside on the porch. A calendar on the refrigerator lists upcoming menus.

On some nights, after a long day driving his school bus and preparing food, Muñoz is too tired to make the trip to Roosevelt and Seventy-Third. But he goes anyway.

"I know these people are waiting for me," he says. "And I worry about them."[20]

What's in it for him?

"People are telling me, 'Jorge, you have no money, you do all this and get nothing back.'" But Muñoz knows they're wrong, because in his mind, he's been well compensated.

"I have a checking account full of smiles," he tells them.[21]

A Preschooler's Project

In 2009, a five-year-old named Phoebe Russell asked the adults in her life why people were begging on the streets of San Francisco. Her mother told Phoebe about hunger and homelessness, and her preschool teacher explained unemployment and other adult misfortunes. Phoebe, in the inquisitive way of five-year-olds, wondered why something wasn't being be done to help her hungry neighbors.[22]

Knowing that her family received money for redeeming the empty cans they recycled, Phoebe asked her parents if she could use the cans to help feed hungry people. They agreed, and with just two months remaining in the school year, Phoebe set out to raise $1,000 for the San Francisco Food Bank.

Before her sixth birthday, Phoebe Russell had provided 120,000 meals to feed the hungry.

She asked her preschool classmates to help her collect the 20,000 cans necessary to meet her goal, a quantity her young mind could probably not fully comprehend. "I thought," says her teacher, Kathleen Albert, "'Five cents a can, one thousand dollars?' It was unrealistic. But Phoebe was adamant about it."

Phoebe spent her recess time each day preparing handwritten appeal letters to family and friends, asking them to give her their empty cans. Word spread. A local newspaper ran the story. Before long, people were dropping off cans—thousands of them—at the school. Others brought cash. Phoebe helped count it all.

At the end of two months, Phoebe surpassed her goal by raising over $3,700, enough to provide 18,000 meals. But the story doesn't end there.

The social-networking website Go Inspire Go (goinspirego.com), which features inspirational stories of everyday people helping their communities, made Phoebe the subject of a video. Inspired viewers shared the video's link with their friends, and soon people around the world knew about Phoebe's project. So donations kept arriving.

After six months, more than $20,000 had been raised. When officials at Tyson Foods heard about her efforts, they named Phoebe a "Hunger All-Star" and donated 30,000 pounds of chicken to the San Francisco Food Bank, in her honor.

Before she turned six—and without knowing the difference between *hunger* and *food insecurity*—Phoebe Russell had provided 120,000 meals to feed the hungry people of San Francisco.

The Kindness of Strangers

On an August day in 2009, Jenni Ware was at a checkout counter at the Trader Joe's store in Menlo Park, California. While waiting for her groceries to be rung up, Ware made the unsettling discovery that she had lost her wallet. The total appeared on the cash register—$207—and Ware was wondering what to do.

Carolee Hazard and her two daughters were in line behind Ware when it became apparent what was happening. Although she and Ware had never met, Hazard quickly offered to pay for the other woman's groceries. A grateful Ware promised to mail her a check.

Commenting about the incident on Facebook later that day, Hazard admitted that she was wavering "between feeling really good, and very, very stupid." But her Facebook friends commended her for the good deed, and they predicted that her actions would undoubtedly generate her some good karma.

At this point, you might be wondering what this story has to do with helping hungry people. After all, Hazard helped Ware ward off embarrassment—not hunger. What's more, this took place at Trader Joe's, a trendy place that hardly caters to a food-insecure clientele. But read on, because it's what happened next that makes Hazard a hunger hero.

Ware's check—which she generously rounded up to $300—arrived in the following day's mail, along with a note of thanks and a suggestion that Hazard treat herself to a massage with the additional ninety-three dollars. Hazard was reluctant to accept a reward for helping out a stranger, so she turned to her Facebook friends for advice. Their suggestion: donate the extra money to charity. So that's what Hazard decided to do.[23]

Hazard wrote a check to the Second Harvest Food Bank of Santa Clara and San Mateo Counties, and she matched Ware's money with her own for a total contribution of $186. Inspired by this update, members of her Facebook community began donating ninety-three dollars as well. Before long, they had launched the 93 Dollar Club Facebook page (facebook.com/93dollarclub), and people from all over the country began contributing money.

Donations arrived in various multiples of ninety-three, including ninety-three cents from a child's allowance and a $9,300 memorial. In its first eighteen months, the 93 Dollar Club raised $120,000 for Second Harvest Food Bank.[24]

At first glance, Carolee Hazard, Jorge Muñoz, and Phoebe Russell could not seem more dissimilar. Hazard is a well-to-do suburbanite who shops in boutique grocery stores, and stays connected through social media. Muñoz is a hard-working immigrant who's trying to help other immigrants preserve their faith in the American dream. And Phoebe is a curious child with an enthusiasm that infects the adults around her. They are three very different people.

But there's one thing that connects them: The common belief that others should not go hungry, not when there is something that they can do to help.

In a perfect world, politicians don't resolve social issues by altering language used to describe the problems. Hunger does not go away because we call it something else; it ends because our country's leaders discover how to use our vast resources to feed every single person who lives here.

But it's not a perfect world, yet. In the meantime, we have heroes like Jorge Muñoz, whose tireless hands-on approach to resolving hunger is getting food directly to the people who need it, every day. And heroes like Carolee Hazard, with the means to write the checks that support food banks and soup kitchens—and the selflessness to step forward when they see someone in trouble. And, finally, heroes like Phoebe Russell, with the childlike audacity to question other people's inaction.

Franciscanomics, in case you haven't noticed, is all about heroes.

A Taste of Charity

To repay Saint Francis for refurbishing his rundown place of worship, the priest of the church that Francis set out to repair promised to feed him. But Francis had devoted himself to a life of poverty and, to that end, believed that he should live as a beggar.[25] So after a long day's work, he would take his bowl and walk from door to door and beg for food.

At first, Francis looked upon the scraps of food he collected with repulsion—the discarded remnants of other people's meals were understandably unappetizing. But once he convinced himself to eat the leftover food, he found the charity of strangers more delicious than anything he'd ever tasted. And he began calling the crusts others gave him "angels' bread."

Nearly eight centuries later, another hungry beggar knocked on a family's door in a small Columbian town. The mother of the house sadly told the man that they had barely enough food for their family. But as the beggar turned to leave, her seven-year-old son brought forth his own plate of food to give to the man.

His mother, trying to dissuade him, told the boy that he needed to keep up his strength for school.

"No," insisted the young Jorge Muñoz. "I'll just have bread."

Six

The Kentuckian

Throughout the ages, leprosy has been one of the most fright-ening—and misunderstood—human diseases. The contagious disorder attacks the respiratory system, muscles, and eyes. It also affects the peripheral nerves, often resulting in sensory loss throughout the arms and legs. But most people associate lep-rosy with horrific images of disfiguring skin lesions that appear as the untreated disease progresses.[1]

Those who lived during Saint Francis's era—who believed that leprosy was a punishment from God—found the sight of the disease's physical effects repulsive. For that reason, lepers—as leprosy sufferers were called—were required to wear bells around their necks, as a way to warn others of their presence so they could look away.[2]

While he was a young man still enjoying the privileges of his father's wealth, Francis shared the public's seemingly un-conquerable aversion to the sight of lepers. That's why, when-ever traveling along the outskirts of Assisi, he deliberately avoided the foothills of Mount Subasio where lepers were forced to stay in collective isolation. Imagine his horror, then, when journeying by horseback down a deserted road one day, he encountered a leper standing in his path.[3]

Francis's instinct was to avert his eyes, to keep from seeing the decaying flesh where the man's face had once been. Surely, he could have simply ridden by, perched safely upon his horse—perhaps tossing down a coin in charity—while the leper stood there ringing his bell. That, undoubtedly, is what most people would have done. By choosing to see those in-flicted as so fundamentally different from ourselves—as sub-human, even—we can easily dismiss them and be on our own fortunate way.

Watching Francis warily, the leper begged for alms.

But Francis was not most people. Instead of hurrying past, he stopped and climbed down from his horse. Walking toward the leper, he was shaken by the stomach-turning sight of the poor man. Fighting to overcome his revulsion, Francis walked closer and was nearly overwhelmed by the stench of the leper's rotting skin.

The leper watched Francis warily. His disease had rendered him unable to speak, and he struggled to extend a weakened hand and beg for alms. Extracting a silver coin from his purse, Francis dropped to his knees and placed his offering into the leper's outstretched palm. Ignoring all risk of catching the ill-ness, Francis then brought the disease-ravished hand to his lips and kissed it. Rising to his feet, he comforted the leper in a long and silent embrace.

In this incident, one of the many defining moments in his life, Francis triumphed over his revulsion toward lepers and, for the first time, became a caregiver to the sick and poor. It was as if lepers—or more specifically, his uneasiness around them—represented all that, until then, had been impeding Francis's ultimate path.[4]

A New Isolation

Today, leprosy is among the least contagious of all infectious diseases, especially in medically advanced countries like the United States. Doctors now prescribe antibiotics to kill the bacteria that cause leprosy, and anti-inflammatory drugs to limit its physical side effects. Even the age-old stigma associated with leprosy is gradually disappearing, thanks to researchers who renamed it *Hansen's disease* in honor of the nineteenth-century Norwegian doctor who discovered its bacterial connection.[5]

With the benefit of hindsight, it's easy to realize that the isolation imposed on victims of leprosy was just as painful as the disease's physical symptoms. For thousands of years, society banished people with leprosy to so-called *leper colonies,* ostensibly so they would not infect others. In truth, isolating lepers was as much about keeping them out of sight as it was about preventing the spread of disease.

These days, though, a different kind of medical isolation is being inflicted upon growing numbers of Americans. Despite all of our medical advancements, tens of millions of people are being cut off from health care—not because they are contagious or repulsive, but because they can't afford to pay for it. And, as if avoiding the sight of a leper, many callously refuse to notice the plight of those denied health care for financial reasons. Maybe it's because they can't bear to see how fragile their own access to health care really is.

Americans overwhelmingly depend on their employers for affordable health insurance: nearly 157 million working-age people are covered under employer-sponsored benefit plans. However, with the Great Recession decimating the former health of their bottom lines, many companies have cut back on their expenses by modifying the health plans they offer employees. Nearly a third of U.S. employers have reduced their range of benefits, or increased employee copayment and deductible amounts. As a result, many families with employer-sponsored health care can find themselves underinsured when a major illness strikes and, thus, legally responsible for thousands of dollars in out-of-pocket medical charges.[6]

One in five workers cannot afford to buy health insurance at work.

Employers also decided to foist the costs of rising health insurance premiums onto their workers. Many have increased the portion of health insurance premiums that their employees must pay. By 2011, the average amount that workers contribute toward their employers' family coverage had climbed to

$4,129—an incredible 155 percent increase since 2000. With their wages reduced or frozen, and living expenses rising, one in five workers who have access to an employer-sponsored plan simply could not afford to buy the coverage.[7]

Of course, many employers responded to the Great Recession by eliminating millions of jobs, which left half of those downsized workers and their families with neither a job nor health insurance. And even those who manage to keep their jobs risk losing their insurance when they get sick; it's standard practice at one in four U.S. companies to immediately cancel the health care coverage of workers who are diagnosed with disabling illnesses.[8]

Health care, it appears, has become a luxury in our nation—one more benefit for the well off to enjoy, and the poor to go without. How could it be that, in a country as wealthy as the United States, so many citizens have become "financial lepers" when it comes to medical care?

Our Government to the Rescue?

In the spring of 2010, U.S. legislators passed a sweeping health care reform bill. When fully implemented, the Affordable Care Act would provide medical coverage to thirty-two million previously uninsured Americans. Under its provisions, insurance companies would have to discontinue their long-time practice of denying coverage to people with pre-existing conditions; adult children could remain on their parents' health care policies until their twenty-sixth birthdays; and most employers would be required to offer reasonably priced health coverage to their workers or face stiff fines.[9] Not since the creation of Medicare and Medicaid in the 1960s had the federal government taken such far-reaching measures to ensure Americans access to health care.

But the passage of the Affordable Care Act was as controversial as it was historic. Opponents especially objected to the act's mandate that all Americans either purchase health insurance by 2014, or incur government-imposed penalties. After much political bickering, the bill passed both houses of Congress—but without winning a single Republican vote. Not surprisingly, after Republicans regained a House of Representatives majority in the 2010 elections, overturning the act became their immediate priority—and the following January, the House voted to repeal the legislation.[10]

With its requirement that all Americans buy health insurance, the bill also raised the ire of legal experts who argued that the U.S. Constitution prohibits Congress from forcing citizens to enter into contracts.[11] Ruling in a lawsuit filed by twenty-six states, U.S. District Judge Roger Vinson declared the mandate—and, thus, the entire Affordable Care Act—unconstitutional.[12] As the political quarreling continued, the issue appeared to be headed for a Supreme Court showdown.

Not surprisingly, government does not have a ready answer to the national health care crisis. If rescinded, the Affordable Care Act would become the seventh failed attempt by the federal government to establish national health insurance in the past hundred years.[13] For every politician who extols the benefits of *universal health care*, another warns of the evils of *social-*

ized medicine. For their part, confused Americans are left wondering whether making health care available to everyone is an act of compassion, or a covert erosion of the free-market system.

Americans are forgoing, or postponing, the medical care they need.

In a cruel financial absurdity, uninsured patients are forced to pay top dollar for their medical care. Health insurance companies negotiate lower reimbursement rates with hospitals, doctors, and labs, and pass those discounts on to their policyholders. Uninsured patients, on the other hand, get charged full price for everything from x-rays to open-heart surgery. To make matters worse, many health care providers—worried that this lopsided burden will result in unpaid medical bills—are demanding up-front payments from uninsured patients.

The full economic impact of the health care crisis is revealed in our country's staggering bankruptcy statistics. In 2007, medical issues caused 62 percent of U.S. bankruptcies—a 50 percent increase from 2001. In almost every case, the debtor had medical bills totaling more than $5,000. Some had lost significant amounts of their income after an illness prevented them from working. Many had already refinanced their homes in unsuccessful attempts to pay down medical debt. The irony is that most should have been protected from such dire straits; they were well-educated middle-class homeowners with jobs, and three quarters had health insurance.[14]

While politicians and special-interest groups wrangle over the merits of national health care, the Great Recession is taking its toll on the public's wellness. In 2009, 15 percent of American adults who were ineligible for Medicaid went without—or postponed—the medical care they needed because of the cost. That figure more than doubled—to 37 percent—among those without health insurance.[15] What's more, uninsured, working-age people have a 40 percent greater risk of dying than those who have health insurance. Annually, nearly 45,000 American deaths are linked to a lack of health insurance.[16]

Although the disorders may be different today, Americans still largely fear diseases they don't fully understand, such as cancer, Alzheimer's, and AIDS. And while some continue to turn away from the sight of people with physical or developmental disabilities, as a society we're making inroads toward overcoming our uneasiness. But we continue to keep health care out of reach for those who cannot afford its excessive costs.

Could there be any more desperate feeling of isolation than being seriously ill but barred from the medical attention you need? Surely, there must be someone with the courage to gaze directly at all that stands in the path of providing medical attention to everyone.

Answering an SOS

On the third Sunday of every month, more than two dozen ailing people come to the Lexington Surgery Center to have medical operations performed. Although the center is officially closed, they've come to have gallbladders extracted, hernias repaired, cataracts removed, and a host of other procedures that they can't afford. The recipients of this care come from Kentucky's low-income working families—people with jobs who earn too little to buy health insurance, yet find themselves ineligible for government help. Or, as Dr. Andy Moore puts it, they are the people who "fall between the cracks in the health care system."[17]

These after-hour patients receive medical treatment courtesy of Surgery on Sunday, a nonprofit organization established by Dr. Moore to provide free outpatient surgery to the uninsured. The surgery center donates the use of its facilities, and volunteer medical professionals contribute their time and expertise. In its first five years, SOS, as the organization is commonly known, treated over 3,300 patients.[18]

SOS clients come from all over the state, some traveling 100 miles or more to get there. Many of the volunteers travel similar distances to offer their help. On a typical surgery Sunday, scores of physicians, anesthesiologists, nurses, technicians, social workers, and administrators give up a day off to provide free care to Kentuckians affected by the Great Recession.

Hospitals, free clinics, and community groups throughout Kentucky refer patients to SOS. For many of the state's 626,000 uninsured residents, SOS represents their only hope for getting the essential medical treatment they need.[19]

"The patients who we care for are the working poor," explains Moore. "They have jobs, pay taxes, perhaps own a small house and a car. But they are unable to afford health insurance."[20]

"As time went on…it became more difficult to take care of needy people," says Andy Moore.

So, on the third Sunday of every month, Moore and his volunteer colleagues offer a heartwarming example of Franciscanomics and its ripple-out effect. By healing the uninsured, they embrace those who, through no fault of their own, have become "financial lepers" in the Great Recession—isolated from health care—because of their economic status.

"I took the Hippocratic oath, and part of that oath is that you're supposed to take care of people regardless of their ability to pay," says Moore.[21] Surgery on Sunday is just his way of fulfilling that oath.

A Family Tradition

Moore, a third-generation physician born and raised in Lexington, learned the importance of helping others by watching his father. The senior Dr. Moore was the city's first plastic surgeon, and many of his patients lacked health insurance and the means to pay him with cash. "He wanted them to be able to maintain their dignity," recalls Moore, describing how his father would accept whatever forms of payment his patients offered. "People would bring chickens or a bushel of apples or a piece of furniture that they'd made."[22]

Following in their father's footsteps, Moore and two of his four brothers also became plastic surgeons. And, also following their father's example, they vowed to treat patients who were unable to pay. At first, hospitals and insurers were willing to help; but Moore says that changed as health care bureaucracies grew out of control.

"As time went on, and medicine became more complicated, it became more difficult to take care of needy people, or even to recognize those who needed help."[23]

Moore had been mulling over his idea of Surgery on Sunday for years, but he wasn't sure how to go about developing the concept. Performing surgery was one thing; but handling all the logistical details required skills that he knew he lacked—not the least of which was raising funds to pay for medical supplies and other incidental costs. Then one day, his fortuitous presence at a meeting helped his idea take root and grow.

Moore was serving on the board of directors for a local nonprofit organization that administers medical care to the poor. In one of their monthly meetings, board members were lamenting the challenge of finding doctors willing to treat gallbladder illness at no cost. At the time, impoverished patients were waiting for up to eighteen months for surgery to remove their diseased gallbladders. That's when Moore described his Surgery on Sunday idea to his fellow directors.

Among the enthusiastic listeners at the table was an experienced grant writer, who offered to approach area philanthropic groups for seed money to start SOS. Before long, she had raised enough cash to get the program off the ground. With money in hand, Moore says, it was time to "stop talking about it, and make it happen."

In 2005, after convincing the Lexington Surgery Center to donate surgical space, Moore began recruiting volunteers. The initial skeleton crew of physicians included Moore and his two brothers, Woody and Michael. Today, SOS has nearly 400 volunteers who take turns staffing surgery Sundays.

"I've been fortunate to surround myself with people whose strengths balance my weaknesses," acknowledges Moore. "Together, we've made this happen."

Economic Symptoms

In a sense, the Great Recession has forced ever-increasing numbers of people in the United States to live like citizens of third-world nations.

"We no longer have to travel to places like South America, Africa, or Haiti to find people who need housing, food, clothing, and health care," says Moore. "In these hard times, there are plenty of people in our own country who need help. And more than likely, they are our neighbors, friends, and even relatives."[24]

Moore points out that demand for Surgery on Sunday's services has increased dramatically since the Great Recession began in 2007. Consequently, the organization's waiting list has grown to nearly 1,500 people.

To shorten the waiting period, Moore is exploring ways to expand the program. One option is to add a second surgery Sunday each month. For that to happen, additional surgical space is needed, and area hospitals have indicated a willingness to help. In the meantime, the organization has developed a how-to guide to inspire surgeons all over the country to establish SOS programs in their states.

Uninsured patients "can't wait till we get some sort of solution from the national government," argues Moore. "They need this health care *now*."[25]

"Certainly, in this great country, we can find a better solution," contends Andy Moore.

As a physician and a taxpayer, Moore finds it especially frustrating when the only option uninsured workers have is to go on long-term disability, wait two years to qualify for government health insurance, and only then receive the surgery they needed twenty-four months ago. Currently, working-age people must collect Social Security Disability Insurance for two years before being entitled to Medicare benefits. The waiting period was designed to prevent Medicare from being saddled with the costs of pre-existing or non-acute conditions.[26] But it also means that a low-income worker with a hernia, for instance, could be out of work for two years while waiting for Medicare-funded surgery.

"It is totally counterproductive," Moore cautions. "Rather than being productive, tax-paying citizens, they become burdens on society. Certainly, in this great country, we can find a better solution."[27]

More himself found one: it costs the volunteers of Surgery

on Sunday a mere $140 per patient to deliver surgical services. By their estimates, SOS is saving the federal government and hospitals around $22 million and $25 million, respectfully, every year.[28]

Rippling Out

Moore has noticed one positive by-product of the Great Recession: an increase in the number of people stepping forward to volunteer.

Why would health care workers spend a Sunday off participating in this sort of "busman's holiday?" One obvious reason is that SOS provides them an opportunity to tend to the working poor—the Great Recession's metaphoric lepers, who much of society chooses not to notice, lest their malady be contagious.

"To me, they are the heroes of this process," proclaims Moore, referring to the organization's patients. "They have endured a failed medical system for an extended period of time before finally getting help. Their thanks mean more than any monetary value you could place on the services I perform."

Like so many others who demonstrate the Franciscanomics ripple-out philosophy, some SOS volunteers find that the organization provides them a way of coping with the recession's emotional effects. "I think our volunteers recognize that *they* could need this help, were they not so fortunate themselves," says Moore. "Many of them personally know someone who needs our services. So they experience wonderful joy in helping people get back on their feet."

In addition, Moore has seen how SOS rejuvenates the physicians who volunteer. That's important, he explains, because recent trends in the health care industry have caused many doctors to feel disillusioned. Health insurers continue to reduce reimbursement amounts, while malpractice insurance premiums steadily rise, and doctors are caught in a financial squeeze.

"Despite the fact that we're working harder, my colleagues and I have seen our personal incomes decrease over the last several years—even prior to the recession. At the same time, society has become more demanding in their expectations of what physicians can do."

Indeed, today's patients set unrealistic standards for their doctors. We want physicians to spend more one-on-one time with us, holding our hands and answering our questions. But at the same time, we demand shorter delays in the waiting room. We also want doctors to be thorough, but we don't want to pay for needless diagnostic testing. And we expect doctors to know everything there is to know about our medical histories, even while we withhold vital information because we're too embarrassed to discuss it.

"I think those unreasonable expectations have caused significant burnout in our profession," says Moore. Research confirms his suspicion; one recent study revealed that one in ten doctors are considering leaving the health care industry.[29]

But Moore takes heart in knowing that participating in Surgery on Sunday helps physicians experience a sense of renewal—and helps them remember why they became doctors in the first place. On those rare surgery Sundays when Moore is not operating, he usually stops in to chat with patients and volunteers. The patients are understandably grateful that he developed the program. But it's the volunteers who express the most gratitude.

"They view it as a very positive experience in their lives," says Moore, as evidenced by the frequent tears shared between patients and volunteers on surgery Sundays. "The patients are grateful for the care they receive, and the volunteers are grateful for the opportunity to help others."

SOS allows doctors one day a month when they get to practice medicine without worrying about the high costs of maintaining their offices or how they're going to get paid. For that reason, Moore believes that Surgery on Sunday has prolonged his own professional career. "This is what I went into medicine for," he says.

Finally, there's another reason—perhaps the biggest reason of all—that Moore believes his volunteers show up for surgery Sundays. They're from Kentucky. "Our population is generally one that cares for other people and reaches out to those around them," he says. "There's nothing they wouldn't do for you, and I think that can be seen in our hundreds of volunteers who step forward to help others in their community."

Dr. Andy Moore is proud to be a Kentuckian. And all of Kentucky—and all of America—should be proud of him.

Moral Hazard

When people know they are protected from certain financial

risks, there's a chance that possessing that knowledge could influence their behavior. For example, a motorist with low-deductible automobile insurance might be inclined to drive more recklessly than someone with a high deductible or with no insurance at all. This potential risk is what economists mean when they refer to a *moral hazard.*[30]

Opponents of universal health care often cite moral hazard as a rationale for limiting widespread access to health care. They argue that affordable health insurance causes people to overuse—and thereby overburden—the medical system.[31] If we allowed that to happen, according to the basics of economic theory, the law of supply and demand would take over and drive up health care costs for everyone. Better for the "greater good," this line of reasoning goes, to let 15 percent of the U.S. population go without health insurance. Better to leave a revolting gap between the haves and have-nots, than to inconvenience the haves.

Moral hazard—and its threat to the greater good—can be used to justify just about any oppressive behavior, whether it's rationing health care or exiling lepers from society. Question is, do the rest of us avert our eyes because we can't bear the ugliness of disease? Or, because we want to avoid looking at the hideous results of our inaction?

Perhaps it's time for our elected officials to climb down from their horses—their high horses, that is—and demonstrate the kind of compassion that Francis showed the leper he embraced. It's the same compassion that Andy Moore and his medical volunteers show the people of Kentucky.

Seven

The Kid Saver

In the early 1990s, Finland experienced an economic crisis that makes America's Great Recession pale in comparison. The Nordic country's unemployment rate skyrocketed from just 3.4 percent in 1990 to over 18 percent only four years later in 1994. During that same four-year period, Finland's national debt grew by 600 percent, while personal taxes, consumer goods prices, and interest rates all shot upward precipitously.[1] As was happening in the United States at the time, Finland had relaxed its lending regulations; consequently, the lure of easy credit overheated the Finnish economy and led to runaway inflation. As if all that weren't enough, it didn't help that the recent collapse of the former Soviet Union—once Finland's largest trading partner—had also caused a 70 percent drop in Finnish exports to Russia.[2]

Nearly a decade later, researchers Tytti Solantaus, Jenni Leinonen, and Raija-Leena Punamäki examined how the Finnish financial crisis had affected the mental well-being of Finland's children.[3] And their findings were universal enough to also have implications for the welfare of American children caught in the fallout of the Great Recession.

As it happens, Solantaus, Leinonen, and Punamäki were not the first to investigate the connection between economic pressures and children's mental health. Researchers have been studying how families handle financial hardships since the Great Depression of the 1930s in the United States. Along the way, they compiled a conceptual model that links family economic stress to long-term effects on children.[4]

Family economic stress has long-term effects on children.

According to that model, parents are the first members in any family to be affected by the despair and hopelessness associated with financial problems. More often than not, the emotional distress brought on by unemployment, income loss, and mounting debt causes marital conflict between spouses. That hostility quickly spills over into the way parents relate with their children, leading them to impose stricter rules and use harsher-than-normal disciplinary actions. With their mothers and fathers directing so much unexplained aggression toward them, kids can't help blaming themselves for their parents' stressed-out behavior. Before they know it, grownups have passed on their depression and anxiety to their children, who begin exhibiting their own antisocial and aggressive behaviors.[5]

When they set out to conduct their study, Solantaus et al. expected to find that the nation's households had counteracted, if not completely foiled, the family stress model—and that Finland's children had made it through the economic crisis just fine. For one thing, they suspected that Finland's generous welfare programs would have helped families through the downturn, financially and psychologically. Furthermore, they hypothesized that, because the recession had inflicted pain equally throughout Finland, families would avoid the stress that occurs during a single household's financial crisis.[6] In other words, society's shared sense of "being in this together" would spare families from feeling economically isolated. In turn, that would lessen the mental desolation accompanying financial trauma. It would also prevent parents quarreling and lashing out at their kids. And it would prevent, in turn, children feeling responsible for their families' unraveling relationships, allowing them to come out of the economic recession emotionally unscathed.

Unfortunately, their hypothesis was incorrect.

Before we look at why it was, it's helpful to know that social research is generally performed using a *cross-sectional* approach, in which data are collected at a single point in time. But Solantaus, Leinonen, and Punamäki had information about children's mental health both before and during Finland's economic crisis. As it happened, in the winter of 1989-1990—immediately prior to the recession—more than 1,300 Finnish eight-year-olds and their parents had answered a survey concerning the children's mental health. Participants were from both rural and urban areas, and from various economic classes. Many of those same boys and girls—the ones whose families the researchers could locate—took part in a follow-up survey in 1994, when the children were twelve years old, and while the recession was at its peak. Possessing data on subjects from two points in time, the researchers were able to conduct a *longitudinal* study, allowing them greater reliability in attributing any changes in the children's mental health to the recession.

Solantaus, Leinonen, and Punamäki found that—in keeping with the aforementioned model of family economic stress—the Finnish recession did, in fact, cause parental anguish, marital conflicts, and deterioration of children's overall mental well-being. Simply put, household financial pressures brought on by the 1990s recession changed Finnish children's mental health for the worse. In contrast to what they set out to prove, the researchers concluded that a child's mental health is negatively affected *whenever* a family's financial situation declines—no matter the extent of society's safety nets, and regardless of whether the decline is caused by a family's unique misfortune or a shared national crisis.

And that discovery has important implications for American children growing up during the Great Recession. Despite government bailouts and stimulus bills, and notwithstanding the emotional camaraderie that failed to materialize from collective despair, the lingering financial crisis has dramatically affected in highly negative ways the lives of families—and, thus, of children—here in the United States.

Declining Family Well-Being

Just how much of an impact the Great Recession is having on American children is revealed in an annual measurement called the Child and Youth Well-Being Index (CWI). The CWI, computed and reported by researchers at Duke University and the Foundation for Child Development, tracks yearly changes in the well-being of children and youth, using 1975 as a base-line comparison point. The index offers a composite of multiple indicators—safety, social relationships, emotional and spiritual happiness, education, and health—each taking into consideration various conditions that young people experience during their first eighteen years of life.[7]

One of the key national indicators used in computing the CWI is *family economic well-being*. That makes sense because, as we learned from the Finnish recession, family economic stress leads to marital strife, harsh parenting, and a decline in the well-being of children. So knowing how American families are faring financially, year-to-year, is important. To make that determination, the CWI researchers consider four key economic matters.

The Great Recession wiped out any economic gains American families had made over thirty-five years.

First, they look at the number of families living below the *poverty line*. The poverty line is the federal government's estimate of the minimum amount of pretax income a household requires to meet food and other basic needs. The threshold varies by family size, and it's adjusted yearly for inflation. In 2010, for example, the poverty line for an American family of four was $22,314. Tragically, more than one in five children now live in families whose incomes are below the poverty line, making America's young people the poorest they've been since the mid-1990s.[8]

Second, researchers factor in the percentage of families in which at least one parent has *secure employment*—defined as a full-time, year-round job. With fifteen million Americans out of work as a result of the Great Recession, nearly a quarter of all children now live in families in which neither parent has reliable employment.[9]

The third factor used in determining family economic well-being is the nation's *median annual income*. The median—or statistical mid-point—income for families with children fell 6.4 percent during the first three years of the Great Recession. In fact, in 2010 the median family income was $49,445, or 7 percent lower than it was in 1999.[10] Harvard economist Lawrence Katz pointed out the significance of that figure when he told *The New York Times,* "This is the first time in memory that an entire decade has produced essentially no economic growth for the typical American household."[11]

Finally, researchers also consider the percentage of children living in families with health insurance. Despite an abundance of publicly funded programs intended to provide health insurance to children without private coverage, 10 percent of our country's children lack access to health insurance.[12]

Battered by the Great Recession, each of those four factors contributed to the decline in family economic wellness—so much so that, by 2010, the economic well-being of U.S. families had fallen all the way to 1975 levels, the starting point for the CWI. That means the Great Recession had destroyed virtually all of the economic gains made by America's families over the past thirty-five years.

If Ronald Reagan was alive and running for office today, he could modify his famous campaign slogan by asking, "Are you better off than you were *thirty-five* years ago?" And as they responded in 1980, most U.S. families would have to answer, "No."

When the Great Recession's final damage is tallied, its fallout will include a lasting and harmful impact on America's families—which includes, of course, its youngest members.

Safe Children

On December 27, 2007—in the month and year that the Great Recession officially began—Sharmaine Nicole Smith exited Chicago's elevated Red Line train at the Sixty-Third Street station. Transit Authority surveillance photos show her disembarking at 6:40 that Thursday evening, carrying her three-year-old daughter in her arms. As the train began to pull away, other Red Line passengers tried urgently to get Smith's attention. Her two young sons—ages six and four—were still aboard the train.[13]

As it turned out, leaving her sons behind was not an oversight on Smith's part. While authorities could only speculate as to why Smith deserted her kids, many suspect that raising three children had become too much of a financial burden on her. Whatever her reason, a few days later, authorities charged Smith with two counts of child endangerment and placed her three children in foster care.

Chicago child psychologist David Anderson uses this story to illustrate how children are affected when trauma overwhelms a family's ability to cope.[14] Increasingly, he points out, parents are dealing with life's distressing problems by abandoning their children to society's care. Regrettably, society's typical answer—turning kids over to an overburdened and coercive foster care system—often leads to further abuse and neglect for at-risk children.

So Dr. Anderson devised another system.

Anderson is the executive director of the not-for-profit LYDIA Home Association, a residential treatment center that helps families in crisis. Headquartered in a working-class neighborhood on Chicago's North Side, LYDIA attempts to protect children by teaching struggling parents how to care for their kids during periods of hardship.

Some years ago, down-on-their-luck parents began approaching Anderson to ask if they could leave their children at LYDIA until they got back on their feet. These parents were without family or friends who could care for their children for a few days or weeks. For many, the only alternative was to surrender control of their kids to state-run custody programs. Under the circumstances, it's not hard to understand why parents would find that option undesirable.

Only half of all foster children are reunited with their birth families.

Although it's meant to protect at-risk children, foster care has historically been the subject of criticism.[15] Frequently, children enter the system after being mistreated at home, and even the best-intentioned foster parents are unqualified to deal with the psychological wounds that result from parental abuse. To make matters worse, news stories expose foster parents who physically, emotionally, or sexually abuse children entrusted into their care. Funding cuts mean fewer caseworkers, which in turn means less thorough applicant screening and limited oversight of foster families. A growing need for foster parents at a time when fewer people are willing to fill that role has resulted in overcrowding within existing foster homes. But most disheartening of all is that only half of the nation's foster children are ever reunited with their birth families.[16]

Imagining a better alternative, Anderson started a program at LYDIA he named Safe Families for Children. He recruited families willing to care for at-risk children on a temporary basis—just long enough for their parents to emerge from a crisis. Once they know their children are safe, parents are able to concentrate on dealing with their own problems, among them substance abuse, domestic violence, unemployment, and homelessness. After they've regained their footing, the biological parents are reunited with their children.

Unlike foster care, which court systems typically impose

after children are abused or neglected, Safe Families is a proactive and completely voluntary option.[17] And, unlike many state-run programs that are preludes to adoption, the ultimate goal of Safe Families is to reunite children with their birthparents as quickly as possible. Because biological parents maintain full legal custody of their children, they can remove them from the program at any time. In the meantime, they're encouraged to visit their children as often as possible, and to stay involved in making decisions that affect their lives.

Host families provide everything the children need—from food, to clothing, to transportation—at their own expense. Amazingly, even though the host families who volunteer for the Safe Families program are not financially compensated, the network has grown to include over 750 families in Chicago and 1,500, nationwide.

"I thought *hospitality* was a term that had been forgotten in our society," says Anderson. "Now I'm excited to see people stepping up and being so generous. And they're doing it all for free."[18]

On average, children live with their Safe Families surrogates for about six weeks, although stays can last anywhere from a few days to a year.[19] But, as Anderson is quick to point out, the child's stay is only the beginning of the Safe Families success story. In addition to providing their children sanctuary, host families also act as mentors and role models to biological parents who lack family or community support. The connections often last long after children return home, and parents who encounter added problems often turn to their Safe Families for help directly.

"It's establishing the relationships between placement parents and host families, in which everyone involved forms an extended family, that is the true nature behind Safe Families," explains Anderson.

Best of all, most families get back together. Remarkably, nearly 90 percent of the children Safe Families cares for are reunited with their birth families.[20]

"Really, all of us can make room," says David Anderson.

Not surprisingly, the Great Recession has increased demand for the organization's help. The number of children Safe Families serves has more than doubled every year since the recession began. Anderson attributes the jump to rising homelessness brought on by the recession; clients are unable to afford rent, and they need someone to watch their children while they decide what to do. On a positive, if bittersweet, note, the downturn *has* inspired more people to volunteer as Safe Families.[21]

"None of us feel like we have room in our time or at our table; but really, all of us can make room," says Anderson.[22]

Indeed, in the ripple-out spirit of Franciscanomics, David Anderson and the scores of Safe Families volunteers he inspires are finding room—inside their homes and within their hearts—for children and families traumatized by the Great Recession.

Long-Term Impacts

Taking into account how prior recessions have affected children, in 2010 the compilers of the Child and Youth Well-Being Index tried to anticipate all the ways the Great Recession would impact our nation's kids. We've already seen how the Great Recession has increased children's exposure to homelessness and hunger, and decreased their access to health care. But the CWI researchers expect other side effects, and their predictions suggest that the various impacts will be enduring.[23]

For one thing, the Great Recession is increasing the prevalence of obesity in children. While childhood obesity has become a growing concern in recent years, more U.S. children are overweight now than ever before. More and more American families are living in so-called "food deserts," low-income neighborhoods in which the lack of nearby supermarkets hinders their access to affordable and nutritious food.[24] So when feeding their households, cash-strapped families in food deserts must often choose between dollar-menu items from fast food restaurants and low-nutritional offerings from corner convenience stores—two options that have been linked to obesity. Not surprisingly, the jump in childhood obesity causes a decline in children's overall health—and, as previous recessions have shown, an increase in the country's childhood mortality rate.

The Great Recession is also holding kids back, intellectually. With state and local governments forced to slash their budgets, fewer dollars are available to maintain educational, health, nutritional, and various other types of programs intended to assist disadvantaged children. Consequently, a growing number of children are beginning their school careers poorly prepared to succeed. Alas, experts say that because those children never catch up with—and, indeed, continue to fall further behind—their better-prepared classmates, they will likely fail to ever reach their full academic potential.

The Great Recession is isolating many young people from the rest of society. Ill-prepared to keep up with their more fortunate cohorts, academically frustrated teenagers will drop out of high school. And with the teenage unemployment rate approaching 25 percent, many dropouts will be detached from their main places of human social connections—work and school. Disconnected from society at a time when police budgets and juvenile crime prevention programs are being cut, young people are at greater risk of getting mixed up in the world of drugs and violent crime.

As if the widening gap between the rich and poor is not causing enough pain, the Great Recession is punishing the most disadvantaged children hardest of all. While child well-being is declining overall, poor children experience rates of deterioration that surpass the national average. Children are the single largest group of Americans living in poverty. And research proves that children who fall into poverty, for however short a period of time, tend to suffer significant and long-term setbacks.

Clearly, outdated government programs are not the answer. Politicians, apparently by their very psychological makeup, cannot forgo partisan bickering long enough to find new, effective solutions. We need to discover creative ways to protect our vulnerable children, or risk losing them to the impersonal jaws of the Great Recession. New solutions—if we're to ward off the lasting effects of the Great Recession—must come from those willing to challenge conventional wisdom and take matters into their own hands.

A Creative Approach

David Anderson grew up in the suburbs of Chicago, one of five children raised to value family, spirituality, and hard work, by a bricklayer dad and a stay-at-home mom. And he inherited an uncommon work ethic from a grandfather who, among his other accomplishments, earned three doctorates and seven master's degrees. But he learned creativity from his father, who won awards for innovation in bricklaying, and showed Anderson that any problem is surmountable with enough forethought, hard work, and persistence.[25]

> # Parents in trouble
> # needed a safe alternative
> # to foster care.

Anderson worked his way through Northern Illinois University, at one point trading a brick-laying job alongside his father for a turn as a city bus driver. Regular passengers on his route enjoyed sitting up front, where they could talk with Anderson and tell him their personal troubles. He would listen thoughtfully as he maneuvered the bus along the city streets, and offer his riders creative suggestions for tackling their problems.

After college, Anderson and his wife, Karen, worked at a group home for boys, and they saw first-hand how family traumas affect children. While pursuing a doctorate in clinical psychology, he worked in Mount Sinai Hospital's child abuse unit. There, he began learning about distressing family crises that—without adequate support—could lead parents to abuse or neglect their children. So he looked for innovative ways to address the problem of child abuse.

Looking to make a bigger impact on the lives of children, Anderson left the relative comfort of the suburban hospital environment and headed off to work in Chicago's depressed neighborhoods. When he joined LYDIA Home Association, the organization was operating as an orphanage. The agency's namesake is a Christian businesswoman, mentioned briefly in the Book of Acts, who sold purple cloth to the well-to-do citizens of Thyatira. After the Apostle Paul baptized her, Lydia invited him and his weary traveling companions to stay and rest in her home, just as the LYDIA Home now offers refuge to needy children.[26]

When Anderson first arrived, orphans lived at LYDIA for an average of fifteen years. Working with the Illinois Department of Children and Family Services, he began finding permanent or foster homes for LYDIA's residents and, over time, he transformed the home from an orphanage into a residential treatment facility. Today, the average stay at LYDIA is just two years.

He developed the idea for Safe Families in response to those parents who needed a safe place to leave their children until they got their lives in order. While searching for a solution, Anderson wanted to steer clear of foster care's notorious drawbacks—abusive foster parents, overcrowding, and low prospects for reuniting families. Convinced that parents are more inspired to succeed in recovery programs when they seek assistance on their own, he also looked for ways to make it easy and nonthreatening for parents to ask for help. And he envisioned a completely voluntary program, one in which parents would place their children by choice, and where host families would open their homes without expecting financial compensation or public aid.

He found the answer at home. He and Karen, with two kids of their own, began taking children into their home temporarily while their birth parents attended drug rehab, received treatment for illnesses, or served jail time. Soon, he was convincing friends to host kids, and Safe Families was born.

According to Anderson, "It's really a grassroots, neighbor-helping-neighbor approach. It's caring people coming alongside those in trouble, lending a helping hand, and supporting one another."[27]

In its first few years, the program placed more than 4,000 children with caring families, and there are now Safe Families programs in dozens of communities around the country. The numbers reflect a growing need, but also the enormous generosity of families willing to serve as host families.

The concept is as brilliant as it is simple. At a time when

families are more and more socially isolated—removed from family and community support systems—Anderson has restored the notion of the extended family.

"The idea I came up with," he says, "is really kind of an old idea…how can we as a community leverage our homes and our resources to care for children of families who are going through a difficult time?"[28]

"It's really a grassroots, neighbor-helping-neighbor approach," says David Anderson.

Rick Wartzman, executive director of the Drucker Institute, a prestigious think tank at Claremont Graduate University, points out that simple solutions are often the best. "One of the beautiful things about the Safe Families program is that by introducing a single change to a longstanding process—that is, using volunteer host families to provide temporary assistance for vulnerable children—thousands of lives have demonstrably been made better."[29]

Underscoring that praise, the Safe Families program received the Peter F. Drucker Award for Nonprofit Innovation in 2010.

The Illinois Department of Children and Family Services acknowledges that Safe Families is an effective alternative to foster care, even though officials there had some initial doubts. Early on, the department's director declared Safe Families a wonderful idea, but he predicted that public apathy would prevent it from succeeding. Today, Anderson describes the agency as "our biggest fan."

"It's obviously very expensive every time you place another child in the state system. Each child we place saves the state money."[30]

More importantly, it saves a kid's *life*.

Saint-Like

To this day, Anderson is still moved by the sacrifices made by the volunteers who open their homes as host families. "People like that are like saints," he proclaims.[31]

Not long ago, Anderson met with the homeless mother of a two-year-old child. The woman was about to enter a drug rehabilitation program, and she needed a safe place to put her son while undergoing treatment. Safe Families was a perfect solution for her; unfortunately, there were no volunteer host families available at the time.[32]

Anderson's oldest son overheard him on the telephone one day, discussing the woman's case and conceding that foster care was her only option. His son, thirteen at the time, convinced Anderson that they should become the child's host family. After all, his son reminded him, stepping up is what Safe Families is all about.

The Andersons had already expanded their family to include their ailing maternal grandmother and a nephew. But they were moved by their son's passionate argument, and agreed to care for the child, temporarily.

Two months after the boy moved in, his birthmother died of a drug overdose. It probably won't surprise you to learn what the Andersons did next: they adopted him.

That's not the way Safe Families is supposed to work. Adoption is not the long-term objective; family reunification is. But sometimes, saints have to get creative.

Eight

The Second-Coat Givers

In early 1209, around the time when Francis was beginning to devote his life to spreading Christianity, he and a handful of companions attended mass together at the Church of St. Nicholas in Assisi. The lesson that day was from Matthew, and it would serve as a cornerstone of his future ministry:

> And he sent them to preach the kingdom of God, and to heal the sick. And he said unto them, Take nothing for your journey, nor staves nor scrip, neither bread, neither money, neither have two coats apiece.[1]

Neither have two coats apiece. The phrase calls to mind a statement from another Gospel source, Luke, which credits John the Baptist with saying, "He who has two coats, let him give one to him who has none."[2]

The symbolism of giving away your second coat—or letting part of your good fortune ripple out to someone in need—is at the heart of Franciscanomics. Indeed, it's what Peter Samuelson, the Hollywood producer and founder of Everyone Deserves A Roof, does every time he provides a homeless person an alternative to spending the night in a cardboard box. It's what Lisa Epstein, the self-proclaimed "foreclosure activist," does whenever she shares her school-of-hard-knocks knowledge with others who face losing their homes. It's what Dr. Andy Moore does the third Sunday of each month, when he performs surgery on uninsured patients who otherwise could not afford these much-needed medical procedures. And it's what Jorge Muñoz does every single evening, when he loads the back of his pickup truck with home-cooked meals and feeds dozens of hungry day laborers under the elevated trains in Queens.

And quite likely, it's what motivates someone like Leonard Abess.

Abess is the retired head of City National Bank in Miami. He admits to having a curious—if not widely common—hobby: he enjoys reading corporate annual reports. As a former banker, Abess especially likes to study the annual reports of banks. And he always pays particular attention to the opening letters, written—or so we're expected to believe—by the companies' chief executives.

"I actually do read the letters," says Abess, adding that he can't help "thinking that some public relations firm wrote them."[3]

Regardless of their true authorship, it has always struck Abess as backward when the final paragraphs of CEO letters begin with a phrase along the lines of, "And last, but not least, I'd like to thank our loyal employees." Why, he wonders, are employees the *last* to get mentioned? So when *he* wrote his CEO letters for City National's annual reports—which he did write himself—he acknowledged his employees first.

In 2008, Abess made a fortune by selling his majority stake in City National. But then, during a business environment in which many banking leaders were demonstrating mindboggling personal greed, he did something remarkable. He gave $60 million of his proceeds to 471 current and former employees.

Abess did something Francis-like: he gave away his "second coat."

Although Abess had been thinking about sharing his eventual windfall with the bank's workers for over twenty years, the Great Recession helped convince him that it was the right thing to do—and that it was the right time. For one thing, he was concerned that the economic meltdown had wiped out many of his employees' retirement savings.

"Some of them had invested their 401(k)s in the stock market. I knew it had been difficult over the years to save," he says.

When deciding how to divide the money among his current and former employees, Abess developed a formula based on longevity. Recognizing that the highest ranking—and thus, the highest paid—employees tended to have the shortest ten-ure, Abess allocated the largest amounts to those who had been with City National the longest. As a result, long-term employees received bonuses equaling as much as nine times their annual salaries.

At a time when Americans were quickly losing faith in the country's business leaders, Leonard Abess did something remarkably Francis-like: he gave away his "second coat."

A Highly Unusual Act

President Barack Obama recognized Abess's uncommon generosity in his 2009 State of the Union address, which the former banker attended as the first family's guest.[4] But Abess wishes his actions weren't so unusual.

"I prefer to live in a world where this is ordinary," he says, regretfully.[5]

To fully appreciate how special Abess's actions were, just look at the growing wage gap between average workers and their employers' CEOs. As we've already seen, many companies responded to the Great Recession—and its long, sluggish recovery—by freezing or reducing employee pay, cutting overtime, or idling workers altogether. Yet at the same time, chief executives at most major corporations saw their incomes increase substantially. In fact, while worker wages grew a meager 2.1 percent in 2010, the average CEO's compensation soared by 27 percent—to a whopping $9 million.[6]

Salaries, it so happens, comprise only part of a CEO's pay. The average top boss's actual salary is $1.1 million—nothing to sneeze at, to be sure.[7] But it's their hefty bonus packages that pad executive compensation. In 2010, bonuses for the chief executives at fifty leading corporations analyzed by *The Wall Street Journal* increased by over 30 percent, the largest gain since the recession began. Robert Iger, head of Walt Disney Co., is a good example. His $13.5 million bonus was 45 percent higher than what he earned the year before.[8] Ironically, while Iger was collecting his excessive bonus, countless recession-weary families had to forgo the costs of visiting Disney's theme parks or buying tickets to its movies.

Top executives defend their outrageous bonuses by describing them as just rewards for producing stellar results. That was the justification offered at Transocean Ltd.—the world's largest offshore drilling contractor—when the company's top five executives each tacked $250,000 in safety bonuses onto their 2010 pay. Statistically speaking, after all, Transocean had "the best year in safety performance in our company's history," according to its proxy statement.[9]

But you might be shocked to learn that Transocean owned the Deepwater Horizon drilling rig that exploded in the Gulf of Mexico in 2010, killing eleven BP workers and triggering the worst offshore oil spill in U.S. history. "Notwithstanding the tragic loss of life in the Gulf of Mexico, we achieved an exemplary statistical safety record," the company's proxy boasted.

In other words, when it comes to measuring safety results, Transocean assigns a tragedy the size of the Gulf disaster the same weight it gives, say, a worker spraining an ankle in a fall—they count it as just one more incident. In the end, public outrage over the bonuses—and the blatant sense of entitlement behind them—prompted the Transocean executives to donate the money to charity.

"Economically speaking, the richest nation on earth is starting to resemble a banana republic," says Timothy Noah.

Abess's unselfishness seems particularly rare among his banking colleagues, especially in light of a New York Attorney General's Office investigation into bonuses paid by the original nine banks bailed out by the Troubled Asset Relief Program (TARP). Attorney General Andrew Cuomo found that executives at those banks—which included the nation's largest financial institutions—continued to accept handsome bonuses even as their companies floundered and required billions of dollars in taxpayer-funded bailouts.

Citigroup is a case in point. Having lost nearly $28 billion in 2008, the company needed a $45 billion bailout from TARP. But that didn't stop Citigroup from paying out more than $5 billion in bonuses that year. Incredibly, the company awarded individual bonuses of $1 million or more to 738 executives. Cuomo described that kind of hubris in his investigative report this way: "When the banks did well, their employees were paid well. When the banks did poorly, their employees were paid well. And when the banks did very poorly, they were bailed out by taxpayers and their employees were still paid well."[10]

In the gloom of the Great Recession, while most workers

face stagnant wages and employment uncertainty—if they're able to keep their jobs at all—the richest 1 percent of earners take home a quarter of our total national income.[11]

"Economically speaking, the richest nation on earth is starting to resemble a banana republic," says author Timothy Noah, pointing out that income in the United States is now more unevenly distributed than in Guyana, Nicaragua, and Venezuela."[12]

Despite possessing a disproportionate amount of the country's wealth, those in the top 1 percent, the so-called "super-rich" Americans, still crave more money. In other words, rather than sharing their second coat, these greedy executives are instead taking the *only* coat of the nation's lowest earners.

Money Addicts?

What is it that drives the super-rich to continue amassing money, long after they've accumulated more than they could ever spend? A study by Harvard researcher Hans Breiter suggests it might be a form of addiction.

Breiter and some colleagues had people play betting games while having their brain activity monitored by magnetic resonance imaging (MRI). When they won, subjects earned small amounts of money. The MRIs showed that making money releases *dopamine* within our brains and, according to Breiter, can produce an addictive pleasure, in some people.[13]

Dopamine, you see, is a neurotransmitter—a chemical that stimulates the part of our brains that processes rewards and creates feelings of pleasure, satisfaction, and happiness. Certain gratifying or intense experiences cause our brains to release dopamine, leaving us to remember the events as pleasurable. So, as it happens, we have a biological desire for dopamine—or more specifically, for the pleasure it produces—and we tend to repeat the behaviors that lead to pleasure. Scientists credit dopamine with our early evolutionary survival; the surge of dopamine produced by successfully pursuing prey—and thus, acquiring life-sustaining food—drove humans to hunt again and again.[14]

> # Many super-rich CEOs are hooked on the emotional "fix" of a big payday.

Often, though, an undesirable behavior provides a person's dopamine "fix." Office employees who play computer games when they should be working, for instance, might subconsciously be seeking dopamine hits—if their bosses aren't praising them for their good work, they might find dopamine-producing reinforcement by winning at online solitaire.[15]

While super-rich CEOs might not understand the chemistry behind dopamine, many of them become hooked on the emotional high that follows a large payday. As a result, they learn to correlate making money with pleasure.

But dopamine's pleasure is short-lived. As the effects wear off, we need another dose to maintain our upbeat feelings. Otherwise, we come down from the dopamine high and feel frustrated and unhappy. For their part, Breiter speculates, the

super-rich must do whatever they can to make more money—
so they can continue to experience more dopamine-induced
pleasure.

Breiter and his colleagues concluded that it's possible for
some people to crave money the way others crave cocaine, sex,
or countless other instant and intense pleasures. But here's the
catch: unless an experience remains new and different, it fails
to increase dopamine levels. So, just as a coke addict must
snort larger and larger amounts of cocaine to recreate a high,
an insatiable CEO must receive ever-increasing bonuses, and
add more zeroes to an already grotesquely large bank account,
in order to be happy.[16]

Call me insensitive, but I find it hard to commiserate with
overpaid CEOs, even those money-addicted executives whose
dopamine needs can only be satisfied by ever-increasing wealth.
Especially when the stories of three extraordinary women—
whose Saint Francis-like approaches to life—prove that pleasure exists, not merely in the act of taking, but in the act of giving, as well.

The Gift of a Child

Becky and Kipp Fawcett sat across from their attorney, listening quietly as he rattled off a list of expenses they could expect
to pay for a pending adoption. There were his legal fees, of
course, as well as the cost of the birthmother's lawyer. There
would be charges for social worker visits and a suitability study
of their home. They would incur the birthmother's medical
costs, as well as her emotional counseling expenses. And there

would be travel expenditures—airline tickets, a hotel room, a rental car—when the time came to go and pick up their newborn baby.[17]

The total estimate came to $40,000.

Add to this the tens of thousands of dollars the couple had already spent on five unsuccessful in vitro fertilization attempts, and the costs the Fawcetts incurred to have a family would be out of reach for most people.

"Building families— that's what we do," says Becky Fawcett.

Fortunately for them, the Fawcetts could afford the expenses associated with a private adoption. Becky ran her own public relations and marketing firm at the time, and Kipp is a successful investment banker.[18] But sitting there that day, listening to the itemized list of expenses, Becky was not thinking of their own situation. She was wondering about those families who lacked the financial resources necessary to adopt a child.

"What happens at this point," she recalls asking their attorney, "to people who can't afford this?"[19]

His straightforward answer—that those unable to meet the high cost of adoption would likely go on living childless lives—broke her heart.

"It just hit me," she says. "I knew how lucky we were." And she also knew right then that they would find a way to share their good fortune.

That was in 2005, when the Fawcetts were finalizing the paperwork involved in adopting their first child. Their son, Jake, now has an adopted little sister, Brooke. And Becky Fawcett has a different job.

Two years later, using their own savings and donations from family members and friends, the Fawcetts launched a nonprofit organization called Helpusadopt.org. The organization provides financial assistance to people who are trying to adopt but struggling with the costs. In its first four years, Helpusadopt.org gave away $360,000 and made it possible for fifty families to adopt children.[20]

"Building families—that's what we do," says Becky, who runs Helpusadopt.org from the couple's apartment in New York's upper east side.[21]

Twice a year, in June and December, a committee made up of trusted friends and associates helps the Fawcetts sort through the applications—and then determine how to award the grants. From the start, the couple had two guiding principles. The first involved money: they vowed that they would never charge an application fee, and that grant amounts would be sizeable enough to make a real difference in whether or not families could adopt. Adoption costs can run anywhere from $2,500 for a foster-care adoption, to over $50,000 for a private or independent adoption. Depending on the type of adoption, Helpusadopt.org grants range from $500 to $15,000.[22]

Secondly, the couple refused to dictate what constituted a "family," a nondiscriminatory philosophy they've employed to help would-be adoptive parents from all walks of life, regardless of their gender, marital status, sexual orientation, or physical ability. "It's just what we believe," says Becky proudly. "Family is family. Love is love. Period."[23]

Adoption is expensive even in the best of economic times, but the Great Recession has put the option far beyond the financial reach of many Americans. "Five or six years ago," explains Becky, "many people might have gotten an additional line of credit, taken out a second mortgage on their home, or secured a second job to cover adoption costs. But now, due to the economy, they're unable to do those things. And that means putting their adoption plans on hold."[24]

Like so many couples, money issues became a concern for Denise Cox and her husband when they set out to adopt. After several failed attempts to conceive using in vitro fertilization and gestational surrogacy, they found their finances strained. That's when Denise began designing jewelry, as a way to help cover their adoption costs. And then, once her adopted daughter had come along, Denise decided to donate a portion of her jewelry sales to Helpusadopt.org, including the entire proceeds from a bracelet she and Becky designed together.[25]

But by and large, the Fawcetts continue to personally provide most of the grant funding. It seems that, unlike the corporate scoundrels who only find pleasure in another big payday, Becky gets her dopamine rushes by helping would-be mothers.

"Creating Helpusadopt.org, and working here daily, has been the most fulfilling experience of my life," she says. "Every day, I am reminded how lucky I am to have been able to become a mother through adoption. Twice! And it is my pleasure to help others achieve their dreams of parenthood."[26]

Becky and Kipp Fawcett experienced first-hand the desperation to be parents. Now they generously give away money—their second coat, if you will—to help build families.

Another Foreclosure Angel

On October 25, 2008, Marilyn Mock accompanied her son Dustin to a foreclosure auction in Dallas. Dustin had just purchased his first home at the auction, and his mother was watching the other bidders, killing time while he finished the paperwork. Sitting next to her, a woman she'd never seen before was crying uncontrollably. The woman, it turns out, had lost her home to foreclosure, and now it was next in line to be auctioned.

The distraught woman was Tracy Orr, and Mock quickly struck up a conversation with her. She learned that Orr had purchased her house in Pottsboro, Texas, four years earlier, and that she had been working on a do-it-yourself remodeling project when she lost her job with the U.S. Postal Service. Orr's not sure why she attended the auction—other than having a vague hope of convincing the eventual buyer to rent her the house. Because, otherwise, she'd have nowhere to live.[27]

"It could be me in that situation," Mock remembers thinking.[28]

Without taking time to weigh the wisdom of her actions, Mock did something incredibly generous. She purchased Orr's home on the spot—sight unseen—for the $30,000 auction price, and then turned right around and sold it back to her for the same price, far less than the nearly $80,000 foreclosed amount.

"I didn't even know what her name was," says Mock, still admittedly dumbfounded at how rash her decision had been.[29] She remembers wondering how she was going to explain to her husband that she had bought a house for a stranger.

Before they left the auction house, Mock made a deal with Orr: she could continue living in the home while paying off the debt in monthly payments. There was no set payment amount—just a verbal agreement that Orr would pay whatever she could afford, each month.

It's not like the Mocks had an extra $30,000 lying around to spend on buying houses for strangers, mind you. "We're not rich," says her husband, Bruce, who fully supported her spontaneous gesture. "We can pay our bills and, if we need something, we can get it." Other than that, they live a pretty modest lifestyle in the Dallas suburb of Rockwall.[30]

"It could be me in that situation," thought Marilyn Mock.

Nevertheless, shortly after helping Orr, Mock started the Foreclosure Angel Foundation to help other people keep their homes. National news stories in the wake of her encounter with Orr generated some early donations. But the foundation is funded primarily out of the Mocks' personal savings, along with profits from the family landscape-stone supply business, Classic Rock. In fact, it was the company's dump truck that Marilyn put up as collateral to buy back Orr's house for her.

Since starting the Foreclosure Angel Foundation in 2008, Mock has helped dozens of people stay in their houses. Thanks to the foreclosure crisis, the organization receives thousands of e-mailed requests from homeowners around the country who need help.[31] Mock admits to often staying up late at night and crying as she reads every one of the pleas. She also confesses that, prior to meeting Orr, she was oblivious to how widespread the country's mortgage debacle had become. Through her foundation, she hopes to inform all Americans of the problem and call on others to help.

As for Orr, she's working again, and now that her original mortgage has been reduced by $50,000, she can afford to make her payments to Mock. The two women, who appeared together on television talk shows and news programs recounting their fateful meeting, are now best of friends.

Why is Marilyn Mock a giver of second coats? "Put yourself in their situation," she says. "If it was you, you'd want somebody to stop and help you."

Giving Away Coats and Pride

As a college student, Veronika Scott did not have the means necessary to help cover other people's adoption expenses like Becky Fawcett does. Nor did she own dump trucks that she could leverage to buy the foreclosed houses of strangers the way Marilyn Mock does. But she did have a couple thousand dollars, and a plan to give away coats—to literally, give away *coats*—to people in need.

Scott was in her junior year at Detroit's College for Creative Studies when a class assignment called for designing a product to fill a need. While her classmates focused on trying to create the next iPhone, Scott set about meeting the needs of Detroit's 20,000 homeless people.

"I have designed high-end electronics," she says, "but right now…in this economy, there [are] a lot of different needs that aren't going to be solved by a new cell phone."[32]

To prepare for her school project, Scott spent time talking with people among the city's homeless population. What she learned from her informal focus groups put her on a path to meet two of their urgent needs.

First, Scott discovered that people living on the street need a way to stay warm during Detroit's brutally cold winters. So, for her class assignment, she created a self-heated, waterproof coat that transforms into a sleeping bag. She designed the coat to use Tyvek®—DuPont's lightweight construction membrane that builders use to insulate new houses against the elements—and wool army blankets. It works by keeping in body heat while keeping out cold air. Scott called the coat "Element S," with the "S" standing for survival.

With that, Scott completed her assignment and earned her grade. But unlike most college students, she did not stop there. Instead, Scott spent $2,000 of her own money to make prototypes of the Element S coat, and then began looking for a way to get lots of them produced. A big break came when she called on the CEO of Carhartt, the Michigan-based clothing manufacturer known for its durable workwear, and convinced him to donate materials and sewing machines. Now all she needed was workers.

Scott approached officials at an area homeless center, called Cass Community Social Services, with a plan to pay homeless people to make the coats. Today, Cass Community employs a group of homeless women to construct the coats, in exchange for a place to stay, food, and a minimum-wage paycheck. "The Empowerment Plan," as Scott calls it, not only gives warm coats to people living on the streets, it also teaches them a trade that could ultimately get them off the streets forever—and give them back their pride. And with that, Scott filled the second essential need of Detroit's homeless.

"The importance is not with the product," Scott is quick to point out, "but with the people."[33]

More than twenty-five homeless people received the coats in early 2011, and Scott and her crew set out to sew 200 coats that summer in order to give them out before winter arrived.

Neither Have Two Coats Apiece

With just 1 percent of the population controlling a quarter of the country's income, there's no arguing with the fact that feudalism exists in America. Super-rich executives stifle the earnings of their working-class employees, thereby increasing their companies' profits and garnering enormous bonuses for themselves. But there is a small faction of people, the richest of the super-rich, who hope to eventually change that.

Led by Microsoft Founder, Bill Gates, and investor extraordinaire, Warren Buffet, several dozen billionaires have pledged to donate large portions of their fortunes to charity. The list includes some of the richest people in the United

States, all of them promising to give away at least half of their wealth. According to estimates by *Forbes* magazine, the group could give away nearly $150 billion.[34]

Of course, many of the billionaire pledgers who have made the commitment to share their riches did so with the intention of keeping all of their money until they die. Still, it's a wonderful gesture.

The United States has over 400 billionaires, more than any other country, and Gates and Buffet hope to recruit them all. By giving away half their wealth—their second coat, you could say—they would redistribute their riches among those who need it most.

In the meantime, amazing people like Becky and Kipp Fawcett, Marilyn Mock, and Veronika Scott are *already* giving away their wealth. And they're proving that you don't have to be a billionaire to make a difference to that part of the 99 percent of Americans who are just trying to survive—and whose standard of living grows ever more distant from the lavish lifestyles of super-wealthy executives who get richer with each passing billion or so paid out in wholly undeserved bonuses.

Nine

The Guardians of Animals

One day, Francis and a group of companions left Assisi and headed toward the Italian town of Bevagna, where they planned to spread God's word to anyone who would listen. As the group approached the city's outskirts, Francis spotted a potential audience gathered in a meadow. Asking his friends to wait for him by the road, Francis hurried into the field to address the crowd.

Some of the prospective converts were standing around. Others were sitting on tree limbs. Many were flying about. They were all, you see, *birds.*

"My sisters," Francis called out to them, "listen to the word of God."

As Francis's traveling companions watched in awe, the birds at once stopped what they were doing and congregated curiously at his feet. They gave the preacher their full attention, listening intently to him as he listed the many blessings for which they should praise the Lord: feathers to keep them warm; wings with which to fly; and the ability to soar high above the earth where the air is clean and pure.

Before long, the birds appeared to be rejoicing. They stretched their necks, opened their beaks, and spread their wings. They began to sing as Francis walked among them, making the sign of the cross. Only then did any of the birds take flight.

"I am very neglectful in not having as yet preached to the birds," Francis confessed as he rejoined his friends.[1]

Franciscanomics is about people who exhibit Francis-like compassion by helping others endure the Great Recession. Certainly, I would be "very neglectful," as Francis put it, if I failed to include those who are rescuing animals from the recession's wrath.

Dominion

The legend of Francis preaching to a flock of birds highlights his special love of animals. That love was behind his decision to protect a wolf and the citizens of Gubbio from each other by bargaining with both. As you will recall from the first chapter, Francis convinced the beast to stop terrorizing the townspeople as long as they gave him food. And he convinced Gubbio to refrain from hunting down and killing the animal if he stopped attacking people.

That love was evident as well whenever friends presented Francis with gifts of live fish, doves, pheasants, or rabbits. Rather than slaughter the creatures for food, he released them back into their natural habitat, often with a friendly caution to be more careful lest they be captured again.[2]

All of these stories illustrate a unique love and compassion that would help earn Francis sainthood, as well as the title, "Patron Saint of Animals." But some religious scholars point out that treating animals as humanity's equals—whether by preaching to birds, negotiating with wolves, or releasing creatures back into the wild—put Francis at odds with an early-Christian tenet, the one that maintains that humans occupy *the* preeminent place in the natural hierarchy. After all, the Book of Genesis, among its "In the beginning" accounts of the world's origin, describes how God granted humans *dominion* over animals:

> Then God said: "Let us make man in our image, after our likeness. Let them have dominion over the fish of the sea, the birds of the air, and the cattle, and over all the wild animals and all the creatures that crawl on the ground."[3]

We typically associate the word *dominion* with concepts of power, control, or domination. But Francis, unlike the majority of his medieval contemporaries, believed that dominion over animals was not a matter of ruling over them, but a duty to safeguard them from harm. So, in the same way that Francis rebuffed the oppressive feudalistic social system of the day—and the wealthy aristocrats who got rich by extracting unpaid labor from the desperate poor—he also rejected the notion of a biological pecking order in which, by virtue of having been awarded the top spot on the ecological food chain, humans are free to exploit the rest of the animal kingdom.[4]

What is it about animals that moved Francis to stand up for them?

For one thing, he considered all creatures—humans and animals, alike—equally worthy of God's love. What's more, he believed that compassion is absolute: either you have it or you don't.

In other words, people who can't feel compassion for animals are, in turn, incapable of feeling it for their fellow humans. Having dedicated his life to teaching God's compassion, Francis went out of his way to demonstrate it personally toward people and animals alike, even though his contemporaries scoffed.[5]

Francis's stance toward animals would likely receive criticism, even now. As author Matthew Scully points out in his book, *Dominion,* the modern-day care of animals is complicated by economics, insofar as their place among our financial priorities is concerned. We still exhibit the centuries-old tendency to put human needs before those of animals—to exercise our God-given "dominion" over them, if you will.[6] It should come as no surprise, then, that when faced with economic adversity, some people are capable of ignoring their pets' most basic needs.

We've seen the distressing impact the Great Recession has had on the lives of people across the country: One in ten U.S. workers can't find a job. And with a third of jobless people out of work for over a year, there is little indication that the unemployment rate will return to its low pre-recession level, anytime soon. Millions of homeowners who can no longer afford their mortgage payments are losing their houses to foreclosure and, in many cases, becoming part of the country's homeless population. The economy's hardships are forcing countless American families to choose between filling their pantries and filling their gas tanks. Between paying their rent and paying for their prescriptions. And, as I wrote in chapter 7, between keeping their kids at home and sending their kids to live with foster families.

People are not the only victims of the Great Recession.

But people are not the Great Recession's only victims; there are an untold number of dogs, cats, and other household pets whose lives are being upended—or, in many cases, ended altogether—because their owners can no longer afford to care for them. Pet abandonment is rising drastically, as evidenced by the growing number of intakes at animal shelters around the country. Shelters located in regions experiencing high foreclosures are reporting corresponding increases in abandoned pets; so many, in fact, that experts are calling the relinquished animals "foreclosure pets." And with fewer people able to afford the costs of adopting pets, overburdened shelters are euthanizing more animals.[7]

Some might argue that, in these tough economic times, people must come first. Scully, the author of *Dominion,* disagrees. Using much the same argument about compassion that Francis made, he asserts that how we treat animals—whatever the circumstances—speaks volumes about our humanity.

"Animals are more than ever a test of our character," he writes, "of mankind's capacity for empathy and for decent, honorable conduct and faithful stewardship."[8]

Foreclosure Pets

Contra Costa County is nestled in Northern California's San Francisco Bay area, about an hour east of San Francisco (a city named for Saint Francis of Assisi, by the way[9]). With Mount Diablo as a backdrop, the county includes such upper-class cities as Brentwood, Oakley, Discovery Bay, Bethal Island, and Antioch. The region's mild year-round temperatures, along with its access to the California Delta's thousand miles of waterways, make the area a popular vacation spot for outdoor enthusiasts. Over time, developers have transitioned the county from a getaway destination into a year-round residential community, complete with waterfront homes and gated communities.

But even idyllic weather and pristine rivers could not protect Contra Costa County from the Great Recession's mortgage crisis—or defend its residents against the ensuing onslaught of home foreclosures.

Foreclosed properties are nothing new to real estate agent Cecily Tippery, who's been brokering repossessed homes in Northern California throughout most of her career. She's witnessed the heartbreak people experience when they lose their homes, and she understands that displaced homeowners are often forced to leave personal belongings behind. But discarded furniture and family treasures are nothing compared to what awaited her in one vacant foreclosed house, on a summer day in 2007.

Inside, Tippery found three starving and dehydrated dogs—a dachshund, a basset hound, and a Chihuahua. In the backyard, she discovered an anxious calico cat, as well as a dead turtle. The animals belonged to the house's previous owners, who abandoned the family pets when they lost their house— and left them to fend for themselves.[10]

With the foreclosure crisis worsening, finding abandoned pets in vacated homes became a common occurrence.

Tippery sprang into action. With two dogs of her own— and a husband whose allergies could not tolerate any additional fur around the house—she knew taking in the animals herself was out of the question. So she called a local animal rescue agency, one with a no-kill policy, and soon its veterinarians began nursing the pets back to health.

But Tippery didn't stop there. She next worked with the agency to find families who would adopt the animals. When the basset hound was diagnosed with a tumor, a condition that renders pets ineligible for adoption, Tippery convinced a co-worker to split the $1,200 cost of the dog's surgery with her. Before long, she had found new homes for all four of the abandoned pets.

As the foreclosure crisis worsened, finding abandoned pets in vacated homes became a common occurrence for Tippery and the real estate agents who work in her Brentwood office. So, too, did finding permanent homes for the animals she and her sales team rescued.

"It's not as if I made it a rule," kids Tippery, making it clear that her employees are not obligated to join her pet rescue mission. Then again, it's probably hard *not* to get involved, considering animal adoption efforts are regular agenda items in their weekly sales meetings. "Luckily, most of us have that connection to animals," she adds.[11]

When the local media began telling Tippery's story, she leveraged the coverage to help increase awareness of how foreclosures are endangering pets—and to find homes for several other pets her team had saved. She began hearing from other realtors in the area who had been rescuing foreclosure pets, too. Now these business competitors are collaborating to get abandoned animals adopted.

"Most people would do the same," Tippery says of her efforts to help foreclosure pets. But *would* they?

The No-Kill Debate

Not all abandoned pets in our country are as lucky as those rescued by Cecily Tippery and her colleagues. The American Society for the Prevention of Cruelty to Animals (ASPCA) estimates that between five million and seven million pets end up in animal shelters every year. Half of all shelter intakes result from owners voluntarily relinquishing their pets; the rest come from local animal control efforts. Nationwide, shelters euthanize two-thirds of the dogs and cats they receive, usually because limited resources prevent them from caring for un-claimed animals long enough to locate new homes for them.[12]

> ## Conventional approaches have done nothing to lessen the pet overpopulation problem.

While the numbers of euthanized pets are staggering, they have fallen drastically since the late 1980s, thanks largely to greater public awareness about pet overpopulation. Around that time, experts estimated that shelters were destroying as many as seventeen million animals annually, and a public in-tolerance toward allowing the deaths of so many pets began to emerge. As a result, spaying and neutering efforts increased around the country, greatly reducing the numbers of un-wanted—and, thus, euthanized—dogs and cats. Then, in the 1990s, a new emphasis on adoption over euthanasia led to a movement toward "no-kill" animal shelters.[13]

San Francisco was the first U.S. city to fully embrace the no-kill model. Under the leadership of local ASPCA director Richard Avanzino, the city launched a number of initiatives designed to reduce pet overpopulation, including vigorous adoption efforts and concentrated spay and neuter programs. San Francisco's model, in which euthanasia is a last resort saved for animals who are untreatable and suffering, or who are deemed vicious and dangerous, has become the national stan-dard for no-kill resourcefulness.[14] The city's namesake, Saint Francis, would be proud.

Saving dogs and cats from needless death hardly seems like a contentious position. But the no-kill concept does manage to stir up controversy, even among animal advocates. For starters, there are those who maintain that, compared with the barbaric clubbing, shooting, and drowning methods employed for centuries, euthanasia is a humane approach for dealing with pet overpopulation. Furthermore, some people argue, even for healthy animals, death is a more favorable fate than roaming the streets, or being caged and warehoused in a shelter. Considering those options, they add, euthanasia is the best way to prevent unwanted animals from suffering.

Even the name itself can spark debate. Some opponents consider the no-kill label purposely misleading. They argue that "no-kill" implies that all animals are accepted with the intention of keeping them alive. But many shelters only preserve their no-kill status by accepting highly adoptable animals. Along these lines, some contend that the name indirectly disparages other animal shelters; after all, the only alternative to being a no-kill shelter is to be a *kill* shelter. The name, then, is a roundabout way of asserting a higher moral ground than, say, an overcrowded municipal agency that can't afford a no-kill option.[15]

For their part, no-kill proponents point out the obvious: the conventional catch-and-kill approach of the past has done nothing to lessen the pet overpopulation problem in our country. And until we as a nation embrace the proactive adoption and spaying and neutering concepts—ideas proven to work in San Francisco and other progressive cities—we'll go on punishing innocent animals, whose only offense was winding up in an overcrowded shelter.

Unfortunately, the Great Recession has dealt a setback to efforts aimed at reducing animal shelter populations. As more and more Americans struggle to make ends meet, many are unable to keep their pets. Whether they relinquish their dogs and cats to shelters, or simply abandon them, their pets will more than likely end up facing death.

The Dog Guardians

Dog rescuer Michele Armstrong cringes whenever she hears the word *euthanasia* used relative to dealing with pet overpopulation.

"Shelters kill 14,000 animals every day in the United States," says Armstrong. "Calling that euthanasia is a disservice to those animals. We're not talking about mercy killing. We're talking about killing thousands and thousands of adoptable pets, and in many cases, killing them in horrific ways."[16]

Euphemisms such as euthanasia, contends Armstrong, make it too easy for Americans to accept the widespread killing that's happening inside their community animal shelters.

"Someone must step forward and say, 'This is not okay with me,'" says Armstrong.

And so *she* did. In early 2010, Armstrong started Lulu's Rescue, a nonprofit organization that saves condemned dogs from kill shelters. Spearheading the initiative from her home in Point Pleasant, Pennsylvania, Armstrong coordinates a multi-state team of volunteers who liberate dogs from animal shelters, relocate them to foster homes, and find families to adopt them permanently. It is, as newspaper writer Amanda Cregan put it, a kind of "underground railroad for dogs," referring to the Civil War-era network of routes and safe houses used to secretly shepherd escaped American slaves to states where slavery was illegal—to "free" states.[17]

Most of the dogs that Lulu's Rescue saves come from North and South Carolina and Georgia, states in which spaying and neutering has not caught on with pet owners, and where animal overpopulation is an unrelenting problem. Some of the dogs were abandoned; many were abused. But all of them wound up on death row, in shelters where unclaimed animals are destroyed after predetermined waiting periods.

"It's all about selling people on the idea of adopting a dog," says Michele Armstrong.

One hundred percent of the rescue work is done by volunteers, or as Armstrong refers to them, "Dog Guardians." They visit shelters in southern cities looking for dogs whose time is running short. Rescued dogs are taken to nearby foster homes for periods averaging around three weeks. With Lulu's Rescue covering the costs, foster families arrange to have the dogs spayed or neutered, vaccinated, and attended to by veterinarians for any injuries or medical problems.

"The foster families help us gauge a dog's temperament—how the animal is dealing with its new life, and how it interacts with families," says Armstrong. "That's information we can share with families who are thinking about adopting a dog."

Next, the dogs are transported north to Pennsylvania, where new foster families await their arrival, and where the process of finding them permanent homes continues in earnest.

Armstrong, who formerly freelanced as an art director while living in New York, serves as each dog's individual publicist. She uses professional photographers—all of whom volunteer their services—to capture the dogs' personalities, and she writes engaging profiles that reflect the feedback gathered from foster families. The photographs and biographies are then posted on the Lulu's Rescue website (lulusrescue.com), as well as on petfinder.com, the searchable online database that matches prospective pet owners with animals who need homes.

"My marketing background helps me 'move the merchandise,' so to speak," Armstrong says, referring to her rescued dogs. "It's all about selling people on the idea of adopting a dog."

The focus on publicity works. Thanks to Lulu's Rescue, more than forty dogs get a second chance at life, every single month.

Like most nonprofit services, the Great Recession has increased the demand for pet rescuing. "We're seeing a huge jump in the number of animals being relinquished by owners, simply because they can no longer afford to keep them," reports Armstrong. "The shelters we rescue dogs from are bursting at the seams. And they're receiving pets that have not had many preventative health measures, such as vaccinations or heartworm treatments, because their owners were forced to cut back on household expenses."[18]

Although they can't save every dog they encounter, Armstrong and her team are making a difference in the lives of hundreds of dogs each year.

Meant for This

By Armstrong's calculations, she spent fourteen years as an "independent" dog rescuer before assembling the volunteer corps that became Lulu's Rescue. She was continuously encouraging her friends and family members to adopt the homeless dogs she found. After leaving New York for Point Pleasant, she tried her hand as a café owner. But looking back, it was if, deep down, she always knew that rescuing dogs was what she was meant to do.

"Dogs give us their unconditional love," she says. "That's why we call them 'man's best friend.' But I often wondered, what are *we* doing for them in return?"[19]

Now, rescuing dogs is Armstrong's full-time vocation, one she spends eight to twelve hours working on every day. It's unlikely you'll find anyone more passionate about saving dogs— or, for that matter, anyone better educated about the country's pet overpopulation problem. Although she worked in marketing and advertising, Armstrong has never been a publicity seeker. Raising funds for Lulu's Rescue has required her to step out from behind the scenes and become the organization's public face. Despite her aversion to the spotlight, it's a role that suits her assertive personality.

"This is *not* okay with me," proclaims Michele Armstrong.

People who meet Armstrong for the first time are often compelled to enlist in the service of saving dogs. Her passion for her cause is that contagious. Friends marvel at Armstrong's zeal for making things happen—and they warn that, unless you're joining forces with her, you're better off getting out of her way.

Armstrong thinks she inherited her spunky spirit from her paternal grandmother, Lulu. When she was wondering what to name her new organization, it occurred to Armstrong that many pet rescuing agencies have descriptive names that include such dire-sounding phrases as "in the nick of time" or "last chance." Looking for something more heartening, she named her organization Lulu's Rescue, after the most positive and up-lifting person she's ever known.

Eventually, Armstrong plans to begin offering free clinics to teach owners how to handle animal behavioral problems that, if left unaddressed, might cause them to abandon their pets. More importantly, perhaps, the clinics will also provide assistance to pet owners who can't afford to have their animals spayed or neutered.

"Getting people to adopt homeless pets is great," says Armstrong. "But we can't solve the overpopulation problem by adoption alone. Convincing people to spay or neuter their pets is the bigger issue."

And in case you're wondering, Lulu's Rescue hopes to start saving cats as well as dogs.

"Gandhi said, 'The greatness of a nation and its moral progress can be judged by the way its animals are treated,'" reflects Armstrong. "I think America *already is* a great nation. However, even though we're the most civilized nation in the world, we still have a lot of animal issues to resolve—from how we deal with overcrowded animal shelters to the ways we raise and slaughter our farm animals."

In the meantime, Michele Armstrong has seen the uncivil ways that too many Americans treat unwanted pets, and she's come forward to proclaim, "This is *not* okay with me."

Pilot Program

The Great Recession has taken some of the fun out of being a recreational pilot. With high unemployment, stagnant wages, and inflated gas prices, it's hard to imagine flying hobbyists fueling up their airplanes for a casual weekend jaunt. These days, most pilots need a really good reason to head for the clouds.

As it turns out, pilots around the country are taking to the air to help rescue homeless dogs and cats from being euthanized. There are nearly 2,000 aviators registered with Pilots N Paws (pilotsnpaws.org), an Internet message board that connects pilots with animal rescuers. Imagine Lulu's Rescue with airplanes, and you'll get the idea.

Recreational pilots are taking to the air and rescuing dogs and cats from being euthanized.

The inspiration for Pilots N Paws originated in 2007, right around the time the Great Recession was officially "taking off." Long-time animal rescuer Debi Boies was trying to save an abused Doberman in Florida, and she was struggling with the logistics involved in getting the dog to her home in Landrum, South Carolina. Her friend, Jon Wehrenberg, a retired business executive who also happens to be a pilot, offered his services.

In the process of helping Boies save the Doberman, Wehrenberg learned about the countless pet rescuers around the country, many who travel long distances to save animals from kill shelters and relocate them to no-kill communities.

"I'd had no idea of the number of animals being euthanized," says Wehrenberg, "and the ordeal people and animals were going through in transports."[20]

Wehrenberg suspected that if other pilots knew about the geographical challenges involved in pet rescuing, many would volunteer to fly rescue missions. So he and Boies established Pilots N Paws to help rescue agencies locate pilots and airplane owners who are willing to transport rescued animals to foster homes and adoptive families.

Aviators can scan the Pilots N Paws site to see if a dog or cat needs a lift to a city they're already flying to; but more often than not, they find a request and plan a special trip to help. And the pilots pay for all the fuel and plane maintenance expenses.

Why are pilots getting involved in rescuing animals? Mike Boyd, a Pilots N Paws volunteer from Broomfield, Colorado, sums it up. "To take my hobby and apply it to help this situation, well, it's just a great feeling."

All over the United States, people like Cecily Tippery, Michele Armstrong, Debi Boies, and Jon Wehrenberg are doing whatever they can to save animals from certain death. If Francis were preaching to animals today, most surely he would list these people—and the thousands of animal guardians like them around the country—among the many blessings for which they should praise the Lord.

A Philosophy for the Ages

Not long ago, Michele Armstrong and a friend got into in a philosophical discussion about pet overpopulation. Her friend, a subscriber to the humans-as-supreme-species viewpoint, couldn't understand all the fuss about saving dogs and cats from extermination. Citing Genesis, he argued that God bestowed people with dominion over animals. And that, he maintained, somehow makes killing surplus pets acceptable.

Armstrong's rebuttal bears an uncanny similarity to how Francis responded to that same reasoning when his early Christian colleagues expressed it. She patiently explained that dominion is not a license to kill, but the human responsibility to guard animals from harm. And, as she often does when she finds herself in these kinds of debates, she shared her Francis-like perspective of compassion.

"There's a direct correlation between the way we treat animals, and the way we treat other people," Armstrong remembers telling her friend.[21]

That was true in ancient times, when the future Patron Saint of Animals preached the Gospel to all living creatures. It's also true today, when Michele Armstrong preaches about the need to employ humane methods—such as adoption and spaying and neutering—to control the pet population.

One day, hopefully, humanity will listen as attentively to animal guardians like Michele Armstrong as the birds outside Bevagna once listened to Saint Francis. And then, all living creatures will be able to rejoice *together*.

Ten

Living Franciscanomics

On a pilgrimage to the Church of Saint Peter in Rome, a youthful Francis experienced firsthand the desperation of being poor. Still trying to discover God's intentions for him, Francis traveled to Rome seeking inspiration among the city's religious idols—both living and departed. The story of his visit to Saint Peter's reveals that it was a milestone in his lifelong journey toward humility.

The Saint Peter's Francis sought was not the grand basilica that stands in Vatican City today—Michelangelo rebuilt the famous cathedral in the sixteenth century, 300 years after Francis's pilgrimage. But the hallowed significance of this church, even then, impressed the young, devout seeker.

Once Francis ventured inside the church, he joined the crowds of people who were visiting Saint Peter's burial crypt. As he watched, his fellow pilgrims one by one placed monetary offerings on the saint's tomb. But Francis felt that many were leaving what—from his well-heeled perspective—were rather paltry donations.

"How can some people leave such meager alms in the church where Saint Peter's body rests?" Francis wondered. Certainly, he thought, the Prince of the Apostles deserved a greater show of reverence.[1]

As if to make a point, Francis took a handful of coins from his purse and tossed it onto the saint's altar. The sound of money clattering to the ground attracted attention, and people turned in curiosity to look at the conspicuous donor. Hopefully, Francis thought smugly, his virtuous act had inspired them to be more generous with *their* gifts.

Back outside, Francis realized that a flock of beggars had descended upon the church's portico. The beggars mobbed the visitors in desperation, tearing at their clothing, and pleading for money. The sight of the beggars' torment unnerved Francis.

"What does it mean?" he wondered. "Here, in Rome, where there are so many men rich, and wise, and holy, is there no one to take care of all these miserable creatures?"[2]

Amid the throng of people, Francis found his attention drawn to the crooked figure of a lone man. Rather than badgering pilgrims in the frantic manner of the other beggars, this man crouched quietly off to one side and simply held out a frail hand. Francis couldn't help noticing all the churchgoers who, despite the piousness that brought them to the holy shrine, walked past the stooped man, seemingly oblivious to his plight.

Francis tried to comprehend how the man must have felt—to imagine the shame of being dependent on handouts from a few sympathetic strangers, and the sense of helplessness as scores of people purposely ignored him. But at this point, Francis was still a wealthy merchant's spoiled son—who in a carefree gesture just moments earlier, had tried to demonstrate his righteousness by tossing a fistful of spare coins onto Saint Peter's tomb. How could *he* ever begin to understand a beggar's humiliation?

Acting on the kind of impulse that caused many of his friends and neighbors to view him as peculiar—if not utterly mad—Francis approached the poor man and proposed an enticing trade. As the stunned beggar contemplated his good luck, Francis removed his own fine clothing and exchanged the garments for the man's torn and dirty rags. For the remainder of the day, Francis took up the beggar's role on the portico of Saint Peter's church. Dressed in the tattered clothes of a beggar, and standing with his hand held out, he did not look like the man of wealth that he was.

That day, for the first time in his life, Francis experienced the daily unremitting indignity that people forced to beg for help must suffer. And it changed him—forever.

Modern-Day Desperation

The plight of today's needy Americans is not much different than the economic hardship endured by poverty-stricken people in Francis's thirteenth-century Rome. Every day, in cities all across the country, disadvantaged individuals stand on crowded urban sidewalks, or at well-traveled intersections, or along busy highway exit ramps begging for money. And like the passive beggar with whom Francis traded places, panhandlers of the Great Recession era tend to take a low-key approach. More often than not, they'll stand quietly, holding makeshift signs—usually hand-printed on discarded cardboard box flaps—with phrases such as "Will Work for Food," or "Desperate Family Needs Help." Occasionally, a passerby will give them money or food. But most people just hurry past, diverting their eyes from the sight of their downtrodden fellow human beings.

The argument that anyone would *choose* to endure begging's indignity is absurd.

The reasons people list for turning their backs on these roadside beggars range from fear to outrage. Some are put off by their desperate and disheveled appearance. Others believe that all beggars are substance abusers, and they'll squander their offerings on drugs or alcohol. Many argue that giving money to beggars only encourages their dependency on others, and they justify their stinginess by claiming that they're withholding their dollar or two for society's "greater good."

My favorite excuse—which I've heard from several generally reasonable people—is the notion that these sign-bearing beggars are not truly needy. Instead, they're conniving participants in some kind of moneymaking scam. These people all know someone, who knows someone else, who claims to have witnessed a street beggar knocking off from "work," only to climb into a shiny new Cadillac or Mercedes Benz and driving away—presumably to a comfortable home in a nearby suburb where they enjoy the spoils of their clever begging ruse.

When you really stop to think about it, the argument that anyone would *choose* to stand in traffic enduring the indignity of begging—and that someone could actually get rich doing it—is outrageously absurd. Why, then, do ordinarily sensible people accept these stories as the truth?

Quite simply, because such an improbable scenario is psychologically easier to accept than the unspeakable realization that, here in the world's richest nation, countless citizens have no other way to survive than begging on the streets. This kind of convenient fantasy also assuages the guilt of walking past without helping.

The Franciscanomics Approach

Francis, in contrast to those who purposely look away from other people's anguish, refused to judge those burdened by poverty. For example, he didn't care how the desperate panhandlers ended up at Saint Peter's church. Nor did he stop to wonder how they became poor in the first place. He didn't concern himself with what they would do with the coins they received, much less consider whether helping them would exasperate an underlying social problem. Francis simply saw "miserable creatures," as he called them, and was compelled to act.

The same is true of Peter Samuelson, the film producer and creator of the EDAR (Everyone Deserves A Roof) portable shelter. Samuelson doesn't dismiss people who are homeless because they appear unkempt. Nor does he refrain from helping those whose bad decisions might have led to their homelessness. When he sees people living on the street, all Samuelson cares about is offering them an alternative to sleeping on the cold, damp ground.

It's the same with David Anderson, the child psychologist in Chicago who founded Safe Families for Children. It's true that parents in some of the families Anderson helps are criminals. In those cases, the children need safe and loving places to live while their parents serve jail sentences. Luckily, Anderson is able to look past the parents' undesirable behavior to see the children who need protecting.

And dog rescuer, Michele Armstrong, who started Lulu's Rescue, doesn't avoid saving animals on the chance that her efforts might prolong society's complacency about pet overpopulation. Sure, she advocates for increased community efforts to spay and neuter pets. But whenever she hears of a sheltered dog about to be killed, all she thinks about is rescuing that helpless animal.

So, what Samuelson, Anderson, Armstrong, and all the compassionate people we've met in *Franciscanomics* have in common is their Francis-like ability to resist judging those in need of help. And that ability, in turn, frees them to do whatever they can to make all of God's creatures' lives more bearable.

If you want to help, but don't know where to begin, then start by bettering one other life. Toward that end, ask yourself what Francis might do if he were alive today and encountered a modern-day beggar standing at a freeway exit ramp?

Start by imagining what Francis might do.

From what we've learned about Francis, it's easy to imagine him pulling over and working out a trade with the beggar—his car in exchange for the beggar's cardboard sign, perhaps.

But that may not be feasible for you. Maybe other people depend upon you—your spouse or partner, your children, pets, or elderly parents. Instead, what if—much as Francis did that fateful day on the portico of Saint Peter's—you put yourself in the other person's place *mentally?* Visualize yourself standing on the side of a road, out of money, and desperate for handouts from total strangers. Picture the scene as people hurry by, pretending not to see you. Imagine the additional indignity you feel as people shout insults your way, or even throw things at you as they drive past. You are an "economic leper," and most passersby are repulsed.

Now picture Francis happening along, arriving at the place where you are begging. It might be reminiscent of his encounter with the leper on the outskirts of Assisi (from chapter 6). Francis stops his car, climbs out, and approaches you. Kneeling before you, he takes your hand and replaces its emptiness with whatever money he has in his purse. He leaves you with a hug and a blessing—and the feeling that you are genuinely loved.

Few people, unfortunately, would exhibit such impulsive compassion today. But consider this, instead: If *you* can afford to drive a Cadillac, Mercedes Benz, or any other luxury car, go to the bank and withdraw one hundred dollars from your account. Ask to receive the money in five-dollar bills. If you can't afford an expensive car, take out a smaller amount—twenty dollars, perhaps, in one-dollar bills. Then put half of the bills in your car's glove compartment. Stuff the rest into an easily accessible section of your purse, or in the pocket of your favorite overcoat. I think you can see where this is going.

The next time you encounter someone begging on a sidewalk, or along the side of a road, reach into your pocket, purse, or glove compartment and take out one of the bills. Looking directly into the person's eyes, press the money into the outstretched hand before you and, as Francis would have done, say something encouraging along the lines of, "Bless you, Brother," or "Good luck, Sister."

As soon as you've given away all twenty bills, go back to the bank and get some more.

Of course, like many of Francis's contemporaries, some of your friends and neighbors will undoubtedly view this behavior as peculiar—and you as utterly mad for partaking in it. What's more, in all likelihood, some recipients of your generosity will fritter away your gifts foolishly, or even illicitly.

So, why should you bother?

In difficult economic times like these, societal problems such as unemployment, poverty, hunger, and homelessness can seem insurmountable. The enormity of these challenges can leave us questioning how we, as individuals, could possibly influence their resolution. Accordingly, the simple effort of giving money to a beggar on the street can feel trivial and pointless—or like a self-serving attempt to relieve our feelings of helplessness.

It's likely that some will fritter away your gifts foolishly or illicitly.

But think of it this way: whatever a beggar's backstory, and regardless of whether begging is a ruse or a last resort, your gift of money, along with a few moments of caring, could be enough to get that person through another day.

And that's a start.

Get Started

Because, you know, a start was all that Peter Samuelson was looking for when he created the EDAR. Now his combination shopping cart and foldout sleeping platform is helping to bridge the gap between homelessness and permanent housing. Offering Samuelson's canvas-covered EDARs gives social workers a new and necessary means with which to engage the chronically homeless. And results show that the ensuing dialogues between social workers and homeless people are helping to gradually steer shelter-resistant street dwellers toward long-term housing programs.

If you're looking for a way to join the Franciscanomics movement, perhaps you, too, could help those affected by homelessness. If the Great Recession has increased homelessness where you live, why not begin an EDAR program in *your* community? As it happens, Samuelson has some helpful suggestions for how you might get started.

You may recall from chapter 4 that it costs about $500 to build an EDAR. Shipping an EDAR to you might require another couple of hundred dollars. So, for an initial investment of around $750, Samuelson's organization will have an EDAR made and delivered to your door.

Maybe you're willing and able to write a check covering the entire expense. If so, that's great. If you're not able to, though, how about persuading a group of your relatives, friends, co-workers, classmates, or church parishioners to pool their money?

"What I would do next," Samuelson says, "is take the EDAR around and show it to the local agencies that work with the homeless population."[3]

Samuelson recommends that you explain to agency directors how social workers in Los Angeles are utilizing EDARs to help break their city's homelessness spiral of despair. Tell them how EDARs are allowing facilities to reach out to distrustful people on the streets who would otherwise refuse assistance. Talk about the EDAR recipients who are finally escaping homelessness, once and for all. Ask your local homelessness experts if they could see the approach working in your hometown. Their responses will determine your next step.

"If EDAR doesn't generate excitement among the people running your homeless agencies, odds are it won't be successful in your community," reasons Samuelson. "If that's the case, then at least your initial outlay will be relatively small. And you can still provide one person a better option than sleeping on the ground."

But if, as Samuelson suspects, you find an agency willing to facilitate a program in your area, then work with its leaders to continue showing off your initial EDAR. Show it to individual donors, community foundations, churches, and service organizations (area Kiwanis, Rotary, and Junior League groups, for example)—anyone who might be in a position to donate money for building and shipping more units. Before you know it, you'll be contacting the EDAR organization (EDAR.org) to place a larger order.

Each suggestion offers a place to begin your personal Franciscanomics journey.

Another way you could help address homelessness where you live is to make your community part of Common Ground's 100,000 Homes Campaign, the nationwide initiative discussed in chapter 4 that is finding permanent housing for tens of thousands of chronically homeless Americans. The campaign's website (100khomes.org) provides a detailed "playbook" describing how to get your city involved in the movement.

Or maybe you could follow Veronika Scott's lead in helping people who are homeless. Scott is the college student we met in chapter 8, who used her own money to develop the

Element S, the self-heating, waterproof coat that transforms into a sleeping bag. Or what if you launched a program like The Empowerment Plan—Scott's ingenious idea to employ homeless shelter residents to produce convertible coats and give them to people still living on the streets?

But maybe your passion for helping responds more easily to the idea of assisting abandoned pets. If so, dog rescuer Michele Armstrong offers a few ideas. It might sound like a cliché, but Armstrong's first suggestion is to write your congressional representatives. "Let them know you don't agree with the killing of healthy, adoptable companion animals—or the use of your tax dollars to do so," she says.[4]

You could also help by adopting your next pet from a shelter, as opposed to buying an animal from a puppy or kitten "mill." According to Armstrong, reputable breeders—those who rear pets out of their love for animals, rather than for profit—don't advertise and usually have lengthy waiting lists. "If you contact a breeder, and they tell you to 'come on down,' they are likely running a mill—producing pets without any compassion or care for the animals' well-being," Armstrong explains.

And, not surprisingly, Armstrong suggests helping to rescue pets—either by volunteering with a rescue organization, or by fostering a rescued animal. "Sometimes," says Armstrong, "having a foster home for as little as twenty-four to forty-eight hours can make the difference between life and death for an animal."

By themselves, none of these ideas provide ultimate solutions for the problems they're meant to address, anymore than giving money to beggars will end poverty. But each of these suggestions offers a place to begin your Franciscanomics journey. And they illustrate the fact that—whether you participate in established initiatives like EDAR or Lulu's Rescue, or have an original idea for helping those in need—it doesn't matter. What's important is just getting started.

Find Your Cause

JobAngels—the grassroots, social media-based employment referral program described in chapter 1—has helped thousands of out-of-work people to find jobs. But, as founder Mark Stelzner points out, the Great Recession has left much work to be done—and not just on the unemployment front.

"Although I'm so honored to have created something that brings people hope, I am absolutely crushed by the weight of the millions upon millions in need," says Stelzner.[5]

To Stelzner's point, the Great Recession has put a heavy burden on millions of Americans. Fifteen million workers are without jobs—and, thus, without access to employer-sponsored health insurance. Three million people join the homeless ranks, each year. Fifty million people don't have enough food to eat. Seventeen million pets are euthanized annually. The statistics are truly overwhelming.

The need is great, and there's plenty of work to go around in order to begin meeting that need.

So, what ideas do you have?

How might you help someone find a job, avoid a home foreclosure, secure a meal, escape an abuser, or get medical attention? What are you most concerned about? You can't change everything, but you could change one thing. What would it be?

Perhaps your cause is rooted in personal experience, the same way that business owner Joe Works is inspired to keep from laying off his workers, and the way that domestic violence survivor Celena Roby is motivated to introduce new laws to protect abuse victims. Or maybe you will discover your cause in a spur-of-the-moment experience—while noticing a group of hungry day laborers gathered under the subway tracks in Queens, like Jorge Muñoz, or while listening as an attorney itemizes the exorbitant costs of adoption, like Becky and Kipp Fawcett.

> ## You can't change everything, but you could change one thing.

Or maybe you'll be confronted by your cause in your daily work—much like Surgery on Sunday founder Dr. Andy Moore encountered patients without health care coverage, and the way that social worker and Safe Families for Children founder David Anderson dealt with families in crisis. As *they* did, maybe you'll conceive of innovative ways to address the problems you see in your daily life.

How you find your cause, or how it finds you, is not important. What matters is that the Great Recession has left millions of devastated lives in its wake, and now is the time to help in your own unique way.

A Broken System

If historical economic trends are any indication, the summer of 2011 should have marked a time of fiscal growth for America. Remember, the nation's wisest economists—the esteemed members of the National Bureau of Economic Research's Business Cycle Dating Committee—declared that the recession officially ended in 2009, two years earlier. Therefore, an economic recovery should have been in full swing. And yet, though many of the country's preeminent companies were reporting substantial profits—and stock market averages were rising nicely—overall, the economy remained in an ongoing slump.

For as it turned out, corporate profits were being propped up by cost-cutting measures—which, during economic downturns, usually involves reducing workforces. As a result, joblessness remained high, and millions of out-of-work Americans had exhausted their unemployment benefits. Government stimulus programs had run their course—with modest success. What's more, the United States had reached its borrowing limit—or *debt ceiling,* as we would learn to call it—putting the nation on the verge of defaulting on its financial obligations.

With an August deadline for increasing the debt ceiling quickly approaching, Americans depended on their elected officials in Washington to do what they've always done in that situation: raise the ceiling. In fact, the U.S. government has raised the debt ceiling seventy-five times since 1962—ten times in this century alone.[6]

But just when the country could ill afford any more economic uncertainty, Washington lawmakers publicly engaged in a poorly timed power struggle. Throughout the summer, legislators held up voting on the debt ceiling as they horse-traded over everything from spending cuts to tax increases. Deals made one day fell apart the next, with rival political parties pointing accusing fingers at each other. By the time a last-minute agreement emerged in early August, it was too late to keep the unthinkable from happening.

Just days after the higher debt ceiling became law, major debt-rating firm Standard & Poor's downgraded its outlook on U.S. Treasury debt, from a top credit rating of triple-A, to double-A-plus. For the first time in seventy years, Treasury debt was not unanimously ranked among the world's safest investments. S&P officials blamed their downgrade on Washington policymakers, who put their bipartisan squabbling before resolving the debt-ceiling crisis.[7]

"It involved a level of brinksmanship greater than what we had expected earlier in the year," said S&P's ratings committee chair John Chamber, referring to the legislative partisanship exhibited during the crisis.

That brinksmanship had cost the country dearly. Washington politicians had squandered our nation's most precious economic asset: the world's full faith and trust that the United States would always pay its bills.[8]

An already jittery stock market, which had been falling in the weeks leading up to the deadline, responded by dropping 634 points on its first trading day following the S&P downgrade. President Obama, who by then had launched his re-election campaign, tried to calm investors by announcing that "our problems are eminently solvable and we know what we need to do to solve them."⁹

Help would ripple out from the kindness of everyday people.

But after witnessing the government's political infighting over the summer, recession-weary Americans put little faith in the president's assurances. And a few weeks later, when Obama revealed a major job-creation initiative, the country greeted the bill's introduction with tired skepticism. The public, it seemed, had given up hope that government could provide a solution that would end the Great Recession, once and for all.

Treasury Secretary Tim Geithner could have been expressing the sentiments of most Americans when he remarked, "We have a political system that looks manifestly broken and makes people nervous about the future."¹⁰

As the nation teetered on the brink of yet another major downturn—a so-called double-dip recession—Americans had reason to believe that elected officials were grossly out of touch with economic reality. And a frustrated public was growing increasingly restless.

A Revolution

It started small, with a handful of protesters taking to the streets of New York City and pointing out an obvious irony: the Wall Street firms that caused the Great Recession had escaped the crisis largely unscathed. Bailouts by their Washington cronies restored those institutions' damaged balance sheets, while ordinary Americans—who despite playing by society's rules—were still losing their jobs, their health care coverage, and their homes. And even, in many cases, their beloved family pets.

By the time autumn arrived in 2011, a hastily formed organization calling itself Occupy Wall Street was garnering media attention. Its members claimed to represent the 99 percent of Americans who, in contrast to the wealthiest 1 percent, do not control the vast majority of the country's income. As their ranks grew, so did their activism, until one October Saturday when hundreds of demonstrators were arrested for blocking access to the Brooklyn Bridge.[11]

No protest was more perfectly suited for a social media campaign, and soon blog posts, Facebook pages, and Twitter tweets were sounding a call to action. New York's financial district, it seemed, was the battlefront of an emerging class war between the haves and have-nots. These fed-up demonstrators were the country's modern-day revolutionaries, and they had just fired the first symbolic shot at corporate feudalism and government inaction. Within days of the New York arrests, Occupy Wall Street chapters began organizing in major cities across the United States.

But, in spite of these long overdue protests, it was abundantly clear that assistance for recession-torn Americans would not be trickling down from politicians or business leaders anytime soon.

However, help *would* continue to ripple out from the kindness of everyday people. It would ripple out from the selfless efforts of a humble business owner in Kansas, and from the networking skills of an HR consultant in San Francisco.

Help would ripple out from the persistence of an oncology nurse turned foreclosure activist in West Palm Beach, and from the courage of a domestic abuse survivor in West Virginia.

It would ripple out from the personal sense of fairness of a Hollywood film producer, and from the home kitchen of a school bus driver in Queens.

It would ripple out from the skillful hands of a plastic surgeon in Lexington, Kentucky, and from the resourcefulness of a child psychologist in Chicago.

And it would ripple out from the generosity of an adoptive mother and father in New York City, and from the lifesaving endeavors of an animal lover in Pennsylvania.

Finally, with your involvement, the Franciscanomics movement will ripple out across our country with ever more numerous examples of ingenious caring. For at the core of the Franciscanomics concept is this simple reality: our lives are bound together through the economy—in good economic times and in bad. And so, whatever you do to help others get through hard times will inevitably benefit you as well—and as much.

Appendix

Are you ready to help Franciscanomics ripple out across America? The list of organizations below—including those mentioned in the chapters of this book—is a good place to start. Many of these agencies need volunteers. Most would gratefully welcome your financial support. And some provide how-to instructions for replicating their initiatives in your community. Or maybe their heartening stories will inspire you to discover your own unique and creative ways to help others. However you choose to get involved, welcome to the Franciscanomics movement!

- **ALLEY CAT ALLIES**
  alleycat.org
  240-482-1980
  A national advocacy organization that establishes and promotes standards for feral cat care, particularly trap-neuter-return.

- **AN ANGEL IN QUEENS**
  anangelinqueens.org
  Provides meals daily to impoverished immigrant laborers who gather under the elevated subway tracks in Queens, New York.

- **ANIMAL RESCUE CORPS**
  animalrescuecorps.org
  Specializes in rescues involving large numbers of animals, targeting puppy mills, animal fighting, laboratories, and other industries that profit from animal cruelty.

- **COMMON GROUND**
  commonground.org
  212-389-9300
  Builds and operates supportive-housing residences for homeless and low-income individuals in New York City, upstate New York, and Connecticut.

- **DAFFY'S PET SOUP KITCHEN**
  daffyspetsoupkitchen.info
  404-345-6821
  Georgia agency that provides free pet food and veterinarian care to unemployed workers so they can keep their pets.

- **EMPOWERMENT PLAN, THE**
  empowermentplan.org
  248-918-9760
  Trains and employs homeless women to produce self-heating and waterproof coats that convert into sleeping bags for those living on Detroit streets.

- **EVERYONE DESERVES A ROOF (EDAR)**
  edar.org
  310-208-1000 extension 109
  Provides canvas-covered mobile shelters to homeless men, women, and children—partnering with philanthropic, governmental, and homeless advocacy organizations to distribute the units.

- **FORECLOSURE ANGEL FOUNDATION**
  To help:
  helpus@foreclosureangelfoundation.com
  For help: helpme@foreclosureangelfoundation.com
  Buys foreclosed homes and sells them back to their owners on affordable payment schedules.

- **FORECLOSURE HAMLET BLOG**
  foreclosurehamlet.org
  Offers online information and networking support for homeowners who are challenging their foreclosures.

- **4CLOSUREFRAUD.ORG**
  4closurefraud.org
  561-880-LIES
  Provides online access to information and advice for contesting home foreclosures.

- **FRAUD DIGEST**
  frauddigest.com
  An online news source that publicizes fraudulent schemes and helps build awareness of mortgage fraud.

- **HELPUSADOPT.ORG**
  Helpusadopt.org
  917-684-5484

Provides financial assistance to couples and individuals—regardless of their race, ethnicity, marital status, gender, religion, sexual orientation, or disability—for covering adoption expenses.

- **HOPELINE®**
  aboutus.vzw.com/communityservice/
  Verizon Wireless program that collects and distributes refurbished phones—along with free minutes—to domestic violence victims.

- **HOUR EXCHANGE PORTLAND**
  hourexchangeportland.org
  207-619-4437
  Portland, Maine, bartering program that allows low-income residents to earn services—including health care—by performing odd jobs.

- **HOUSING FIRST**
  c/o PATHWAYS TO HOUSING
  pathwaystohousing.org
  212-289-0000
  Provides housing to people who are homeless, and then adds supportive services in the areas of mental and physical health, substance abuse, education, and employment.

- **JOBANGELS PROGRAM**
  c/o HIRING FOR HOPE
  hiringforhope.org
  404-920-8636
  A grassroots networking program working to bring together people who share a commitment to helping others find gainful employment.

- **LETHALITY ASSESSMENT PROGRAM c/o MARYLAND NETWORK AGAINST DOMESTIC VIOLENCE (MNADV)**
  mnadv.org/lethality.html
  301-352-4574
  An eleven-question risk-assessment checklist that helps law enforcement officers spot factors known to contribute to domestic violence-related homicides.

- **LULU'S RESCUE**
  lulusrescue.com
  Rescues healthy animals that are slated to die in shelters, and finds them permanent homes.

- **NATIONAL NETWORK TO END DOMESTIC VIOLENCE (NNEDV)**
  nnedv.org
  202-543-5566
  Offers programs and initiatives that address the causes and consequences of domestic violence and intimate partner abuse.

- **93 DOLLAR CLUB**
  facebook.com/93dollarclub
  Inspired by a woman's neighborly act in a grocery store, this Facebook group raises money for Second Harvest Food Bank.

- **100,000 HOMES CAMPAIGN**
  100khomes.org
  A national movement of communities attempting to find permanent homes for one hundred thousand of America's most vulnerable homeless individuals and families.

- **ONE WORLD EVERYBODY EATS FOUNDATION**
  oneworldeverybodyeatsfoundation.org
  801-953-9953
  Helps communities establish pay-what-you-can cafés, with no set menus or stated prices, and where customers have the option to exchange work for meals.

- **PILOTS N PAWS**
  pilotsnpaws.org
  An Internet message board that connects pilots with animal rescuers, with the intention of transporting doomed pets to no-kill communities.

- **SAFE FAMILIES FOR CHILDREN c/o LYDIA HOME ASSOCIATION**
  safe-families.org
  A network of families that take in at-risk children on a temporary basis, giving their parents time to deal with a personal crisis.

- **SURGERY ON SUNDAYS**
  surgeryonsunday.org
  859-246-0046
  Medical professionals who volunteer their time and skills to provide free outpatient surgery to Kentucky's uninsured.

- **TIANA ANGELIQUE NOTICE MEMORIAL FOUNDATION**
  tiananoticefoundation.org
  Installs video cameras outside the homes of domestic violence victims, to help identify and prosecute their abusers.

- **WEST VIRGINIA COALITION AGAINST DOMESTIC VIOLENCE**
  wvcadv.org
  304-965-3552
  A statewide alliance of community-based domestic violence programs.

- **WE'VE GOT TIME TO HELP**
  wevegottimetohelp.org
  Matches unemployed volunteers with people who need assistance, from fixing leaky faucets to helping families move.

- **WORTH OUR WEIGHT**
  worthourweight.org
  707-544-1200
  Santa Rosa, California, apprentice program that provides tuition-free culinary and foodservice training to at-risk young people.

Notes

Introduction: Shattered Faith and Renewed Hope

1. "History of the NBER," National Bureau of Economic Research, accessed August 23, 2010, http://www.nber.org/info.html.
2. Sewell Chan, "U.S. Economist Dissents, Saying Recession Is Over," *New York Times,* April 13, 2010.
3. "NBER Committee Confers: No Trough Announced," National Bureau of Economic Research, accessed August 23, 2010, http://www.nber.org/cycles /april2010.html.
4. Chan, "U.S. Economist Dissents."
5. Iwan J. Azis, "Predicting a Recovery Date from the Economic Crisis of 2008," *Socio-Economic Planning Sciences* (September 2010): 122-129.
6. Sudeep Reddy and Nick Timiraos, "Plunge in Home Sales Stokes Economy Fears," *The Wall Street Journal,* August 25, 2010.
7. Azis, "Predicting a Recovery Date."
8. "Timeline: A Year of Financial Crisis," NPR, accessed August 25, 2010, http://www.npr.org/templates/story/story.php?storyId=112538025.
9. Steven Rattner, "After Bankruptcy, GM, Chrysler Turn the Corner," *The Washington Post,* June 1, 2010, http://www.washingtonpost.com /wp-dyn/content/article/2010/05/31/AR2010053101642.html.
10. "Timeline: A Year of Financial Crisis," NPR.
11. Michael R. Critttenden, "FDIC Finds 829 U.S. Banks at Risk," *The Wall Street Journal,* September 1, 2010.
12. "Timeline: A Year of Financial Crisis," NPR.
13. Peter A. McKay, "Dow Is Off 7,401.24 Points From Its Record High in '07," *The Wall Street Journal,* March 3, 2009.
14. "Labor Force Statistics from the Current Population Survey," Bureau of Labor Statistics, accessed August 25, 2010, http://data.bls.gov/PDQ/servlet /SurveyOutputServlet?data_tool=latest_numbers&series_id=NS14000000.

15. Bureau of Labor Statistics, "The Employment Situation—July 2010," news release, August 6, 2010.

16. Dennis Jacobe, "U.S. Underemployment at 18.3% in Mid-August," *Gallup,* August 17, 2010, http://www.gallup.com/poll/142169/Underemployment-Mid-August.aspx.

17. Walter Brandimarte, "Euro Hit Again By Debt Jitters; Stocks Seesaw," *Reuters,* May 24, 2010, http://www.reuters.com/article /idUSN24255826 20100524.

18. Chan, "U.S. Economist Dissents."

19. Matthew Benjamin, "Volcker Says U.S., World in a 'Great Recession,'" *Bloomberg,* April 23, 2009, http://www.bloomberg.com/apps/news?pid= newsarchive&sid=ainh3qdHJuoM.

20. "NBER Business Cycle Dating Committee Announces Trough Date," National Bureau of Economic Research, accessed September 20, 2010, http://www.nber.org/cycles/sept2010.html.

21. Kevin G. Hall, "Great Recession Ended in June 2009, But Who Knew?" *The Miami Herald,* September 20, 2010.

22. Bob Willis, "U.S. Recession Worst Since Great Depression, Revised Data Show," *Bloomberg,* August 1, 2009, http://www.bloomberg.com/apps /news?pid=newsarchive&sid=aNivTjr852TI.

23. W. Carl Biven, *Jimmy Carter's Economy: Policy in an Age of Limits* (Chapel Hill, NC: University of North Carolina Press, 2002), 1-14.

24. "Prime Rate History," WSJ Prime Rate, accessed August 30, 2010, http://wsjprimerate.us/wall_street_journal_prime_rate_history.htm.

25. Reddy and Timiraos, "Plunge in Home Sales Stokes Economy Fears."

26. "Historical US Inflation Rate 1914-Present," InflationData.com, accessed August 30, 2010, http://inflationdata.com/inflation/Inflation_Rate /HistoricalInflation.aspx?dsInflation_currentPage=2.

27. "Labor Force Statistics," Bureau of Labor Statistics.

28. Ron Nessen, "The Brookings Instituition's Arthur Okun—Father of the 'Misery Index,'" The Brookings Institution, accessed August 30, 2010, http://www.brookings.edu/opinions/2008/1217_misery_index_nessen .aspx.

29. Bret Schulte, "Ronald Reagan v. Jimmy Carter: 'Are You Better Off Than You Were Four Years Ago?'" *U.S. News & World Report,* January 17, 2008, http://politics.usnews.com/news/politics/articles/2008/01/17/the-actor-and-the-detail-man.html.

30. "United States Presidential Election Results," Atlas of U.S. Presidential Elections, accessed August 31, 2010, http://uselectionatlas.org/RESULTS/.

31. Stewart Hamilton and Alicia Micklethwait, *Greed and Corporate Failure: The Lessons from Recent Disasters.* (New York: Palgrave Macmillan, 2006), 81-97.

32. Ibid.

33. Anthony Bianco et al., "The Rise and Fall of Dennis Kozlowski," *Business Week Online,* December 23, 2002, http://www.businessweek.com /magazine/content/02_51/b3813001.htm.

34. Bloomberg News, "Kozlowski Building Is Renamed At Seton Hall," *The Baltimore Sun,* August 19, 2005.

35. Kara Scannell, "Citi's Pact With SEC Is Held Up By Judge," *The Wall Street Journal,* August 17, 2010.

36. Peter Whoriskey, "AIG Spa Trip Fuels Fury On Hill," *The Washington Post,* October 8, 2008.

37. Karey Wutkowski, "Auto Execs' Private Flights to Washington Draw Ire," *Reuters,* November 19, 2008, http://www.reuters.com/article /idUSTRE4AI8C520081119.

38. Ann Gerhart, "BP Chairman Talks About The 'Small People,' Further Angering Gulf," *The Washington Post,* June 17, 2010.

39. Wharton School, "Why Smart People Do Unethical Things: What's Behind Another Year of Corporate Scandals," knowledge@wharton.com (January 14, 2004), http://knowledge.wharton.upenn.edu/article.cfm ?articleid=911.

40. Ibid.

41. Michael Prestwich, "Feudalism," in *The Social Science Encyclopedia,* 2nd ed., eds. Adam Kuper and Jessica Kuper (New York: Routledge, 1996), 300-301.

42. Philippe Aghion and Patrick Bolton, "A Theory of Trickle-Down Growth and Development," *The Review of Economic Studies* 64, no. 2 (1997): 151-172.

43. Ibid.

44. Andrew E. Busch, *Ronald Reagan and the Politics of Freedom* (Lanham, MA: Rowman & Littlefield, 2001), 82-87.

45. Murray Bodo, *The Threefold Way of Saint Francis* (Mahwah, NJ: Paulist, 2000), 12.

46. Edmund O'Gorman, *St. Francis For Today,* rev. ed. (Leominster, Herefordshire, England: Gracewing, 1996), 21-27.

47. Father Cuthbert, "Professor Harnack and the Gospel," *Catholic World,* February 1904, 603-616.

48. John Gouch, "Furlough Relief Fund Will Assist 158 Employees," Clemson University, accessed September 2, 2010, http://www.clemson.edu /newsroom/articles/2009/january/furlough_fund.php5.

49. Dana Mattioli and Sara Murray, "Employers Hit Salaried Staff With Furloughs," *The Wall Street Journal,* February 24, 2009.

One: A Job Angel and a Thoughtful Man

1. *The Little Flowers of Saint Francis,* trans. Thomas Okey (Mineola, NY: Dover Publications, 2003).
2. Sara Murray, "Slump Over, Pain Persists," *The Wall Street Journal,* September 21, 2010.
3. Sara Murray and Phil Izzo, "Job Search Stretches Past a Year for Millions, *The Wall Street Journal,* July 22, 2011.
4. CareerBuilder, "Over Half of Unemployed Workers With Job Offers Said the Pay Was More Than 25 Percent Below Previous Salary, New Personified Survey Finds," news release, September 23, 2010, http://www.prnewswire.com/news-releases/over-half-of-unemployed-workers-with-job-offers-said-the-pay-was-more-than-25-percent-below-previous-salary-new-personified-survey-finds-103607579.html.
5. Motoko Rich, "For the Unemployed Over 50, Fears of Never Working Again," *The New York Times,* September 19, 2010.
6. "2009/2010 Looking Toward Recovery: Focusing on Talent and Rewards," Towers Watson, accessed September 14, 2010, http://www.worldatwork.org/waw/adimLink?id=34555.
7. Chris Isidore, "Job Loss: Worst in 34 Years," CNNMoney.com, accessed September 14, 2010, http://money.cnn.com/2009/02/06/news/economy/jobs_january/index.htm.
8. Laura Raines, "Grass-Roots 'Angels' Help Connect Seekers, Jobs," *The Atlanta Journal-Constitution,* June 28, 2009.
9. Mark Stelzner, "How JobAngels (And You) Have Changed My Life," *JobAngels Blog,* February 1, 2010, http://www.jobangels.org/JobAngels-Blog/How-JobAngels-And-You-Have-Changed-My-Life.html.
10. Sarah E. Needleman, "Strangers Lend a Hand to Job Seekers," *The Wall Street Journal,* March 24, 2009.
11. Mark Stelzner (founder, JobAngels), in e-mail discussions with the author, September 2010.
12. Stelzner, "How JobAngels."
13. Mark Stelzner, e-mail discussions.
14. Kevin Tibbles, "Sharing the Wealth," *The Daily Nightly* (blog), March 16, 2009, http://dailynightly.msnbc.msn.com/_news/2009/03/16/4372432-sharing-the-wealth?pc=25&sp=25.
15. Bob Johnson, "B&W Labor Benefits Community," *The Iola Register,* March 7, 2009.

16. Joe Works (owner, B&W Trailer Hitches), in e-mail discussions with the author, September 2010.
17. Martin L. Hoffman, "Empathy and Justice Motivation," *Motivation and Emotion* 14, no. 2 (1990): 151-172.
18. Abraham Sagi and Martin L. Hoffman, "Empathic Distress in the Newborn," *Developmental Psychology* 12, no. 2 (1976): 175-176.
19. Hisashi Nakao and Shoji Itakura, "An Integrated View of Empathy: Psychology, Philosophy, and Neuroscience," *Integrative Psychological and Behavioral Science* 43, no. 1 (2009): 42-52.
20. Hoffman, "Empathy and Justice Motivation."
21. Daniel C. Batson, "Self-Other Merging and the Empathy-Altruism Hypothesis," *Journal of Personality and Social Psychology* 73, no. 3 (1997): 517-522.
22. Daniel C. Batson, "How Social an Animal?" *American Psychologist* 45, no. 3 (1990): 336-346.
23. John M. Darley and C. Daniel Batson, "'From Jerusalem to Jericho': A Study of Situational and Dispositional Variables in Helping Behavior," *Journal of Personality and Social Psychology* 27, no. 1 (1973): 100-108.
24. Joe Works, e-mail discussions.
25. Tibbles, "Sharing the Wealth."
26. Joe Works, e-mail discussions.
27. Mark Stelzner, e-mail discussions.
28. Hiring for Hope, "Two Nonprofits Merge to Better Assist Job Seekers," news release, February 28, 2011, http://www.hiringforhope.org/pdf /HFH-JA%20Press%20ReleaseFinal%202-11.pdf.
29. Karen Caffarini, "Boston Physicians Cut Their Own Salaries To Help Hospital," amednews.com (April 6, 2009), http://www.ama-assn.org /amednews/2009/04/06/bisc0406.htm.
30. Victoria Staff Elliott, "Boston Hospital Giving Raises Again; Doctors Took Pay Cut," amednews.com (March 1, 2010), http://www.ama-assn.org /amednews/2010/03/01/bisc0301.htm.
31. Medical University of South Carolina, "MUSC Fund Raises More Than $175,000 For Employee Relief," news release, February 4, 2009, http://www.musc.edu/pr/furlough_fund.htm.
32. Nancy Woods, "Job Loss Leads Man to Form Thriving Organization," KATU.com (May 6, 2009), http://www.katu.com/economy/44411887 .html.
33. Arthur Delaney, "Gene Epstein, Philanthropist, Will Donate $1,000 To Charity Every Time a Business Hires an Unemployed Person," *The Huffington Post* (blog), September 9, 2010, http://www.huffingtonpost.com /2010/09/09/white-house-pushes-fiscal_n_709493.html.

Two: The Foreclosure Activist

1. Robyn Powell, in telephone discussion with the author, October 2010.
2. Tony Pugh, "Civilian Watchdogs Saw Shady Mortgage Work," *Concord Monitor,* October 20, 2010.
3. Lisa Epstein (founder, ForeclosureHamlet.org), in telephone discussion with the author, October 2010.
4. Tamara Draut and Jose Garcia, "Unfairness in Life and Lending: Credit and Low-Income Americans," paper presented at Moving Forward: The Future of Consumer Credit and Mortgage Finance—A National Symposium, Boston, MA, February 2010, http://www.jchs.harvard.edu /publications/MF10-1.pdf.
5. Eric S. Belsky and Nela Richardson, "Understanding the Boom and Bust in Nonprime Mortgage Lending," Joint Center for Housing Studies of Harvard University, September 2010, http://www.jchs.harvard.edu /publications/finance/UBB10-1.pdf.
6. Ibid.
7. Ellen Schloemer, Wei Li, Keith Ernst, and Kathleen Keest, "Losing Ground: Foreclosures in the Subprime Market and Their Cost to Homeowners," Center for Responsible Lending, accessed October 22, 2010, http://www.responsiblelending.org/mortgage-lending/research-analysis /foreclosure-paper-report-2-17.pdf.
8. Tony Schwartz, "Dope, Dopes, and Dopamine: The Problem With Money," *Fast Company Expert Blog,* October 27, 2010, http: //www.fastcompany.com/1698302/dope-dopes-and-dopamine-the-problem-with-money.
9. Lisa Epstein to Florida Supreme Court Justices, October 7, 2009, Florida Supreme Court, http://www.floridasupremecourt.org/pub_info /documents/foreclosure_comments/Filed_10-07-2009_Epstein.pdf.
10. Lisa Epstein, telephone discussion.
11. Robbie Whelan, "Niche Lawyers Spawned Housing Fracas," *The Wall Street Journal,* October 21, 2010.
12. David McLaughlin, "Why Florida's Foreclosure Machine Is Slowing Down," *BusinessWeek,* October 13, 2010.
13. Paola Iuspa-Abbott, "Housing Meltdown," *4closureFraud* (blog), September 7, 2010, http://4closurefraud.org/2010/09/07/exclusive-expose-housing-meltdown-4closurefraud-org-and-foreclosurehamlet-org-featured-in-the-daily-business-review/.
14. Pugh, "Civilian Watchdogs."
15. Vanessa O'Connell, "One Probe, 50 States, High Stakes," *The Wall Street Journal,* November 1, 2010.

16. Kimberly Miller, "'Deadbeat' Fights Back Against Foreclosure Process," *The Palm Beach Post,* October 19, 2010.

17. Lisa Epstein, telephone discussion.

18. Martha Stout, *The Sociopath Next Door: The Ruthless Versus the Rest of Us* (New York: Broadway Books, 2005), 106.

Three: The Stigma Fighters

1. Michael Robson, *St Francis of Assisi: The Legend and the Life* (New York: Continuum, 1999), 262-264.

2. Valerie Martin, "Being Saint Francis," *Atlantic Monthly* 286, no. 2 (2000): 52-61.

3. Robert Kiely, "Further Considerations of the Holy Stigmata of St. Francis: Where Was Brother Leo?" *Religion & The Arts* 3, no. 1 (1999): 20-40.

4. Celena Roby, in e-mail discussions with the author, December 2010.

5. Jonay Corley, "Victim Seeks to Change State Laws," *Tyler Star News,* December 8, 2010.

6. "Domestic Violence Counts 2008: A 24-Hour Census of Domestic Violence Shelters and Services," National Network to End Domestic Violence, accessed November 22, 2010, http://www.nnedv.org /docs/Census/DVCounts2008/DVCounts08_Report_Color.pdf.

7. Erica L. Smith and Donald J. Farole, Jr., "Profile of Intimate Partner Violence Cases in Large Urban Counties," *Bureau of Justice Statistics Special Report,* October 2009, http://bjs.ojp.usdoj.gov/content/pub/pdf /pipvcluc.pdf.

8. Ibid.

9. "Frequently Asked Questions About Domestic Violence," National Network to End Domestic Violence, accessed December 7, 2010, http://www.nnedv.org/docs/Stats/NNEDV_FAQaboutDV2010.pdf.

10. Kenneth Corvo and Ellen deLara, "Towards an Integrated Theory of Relational Violence: Is Bullying a Risk Factor for Domestic Violence?" *Aggression and Violent Behavior* 15, no. 3 (2010): 181-190.

11. Claire M. Renzetti, "Economic Stress and Domestic Violence," with contributions by Vivian M. Larkin, The National Online Resource Center on Violence Against Women, September 2009, http://new.vawnet.org /Assoc_Files_VAWnet/AR_EconomicStress.pdf.

12. "The Impact of the Economy on Domestic Violence," National Network to End Domestic Violence, accessed November 22, 2010, http://www.nrcdv.org/dvam/docs/materials/09-resource-packet /Issue_FactSheets_Handouts/ImpactofEconomy_FactSheet.pdf.

13. Renzetti, "Economic Stress and Domestic Violence."

14. Ibid.

15. "The Impact of the Economy on Domestic Violence."

16. Corley, "Victim Seeks to Change State Laws."

17. Office of the Governor Earl Ray Tomblin, "Governor Tomblin Signs 'Celena's Law,'" press release, March 24, 2011, http://www.governor.wv.gov/newsroom/pressreleases/Pages/GovernorTomblinSignsCelena'sLaw.aspx.

18. Ibid.

19. Celena Roby, e-mail discussions.

20. "Providing a Life-Line in Pittsburgh—Crisis Center North," Verizon Wireless, accessed December 15, 2010, http://aboutus.vzw.com/communityservice/casestudypitt.html.

21. "HopeLine Press Kit," Verizon Wireless, accessed October 14, 2011, http://aboutus.vzw.com/communityservice/Hopeline_PressKit.pdf.

22. "About the Hotline," The National Domestic Violence Hotline, accessed December 15, 2010, http://www.thehotline.org/about-support/.

23. "Deceased Alum's Life Featured in Domestic Violence Documentary," *The Daily Collegian,* June 7, 2010.

24. Rebecca Kanable, "Learning to Read the Danger Signs," *Law Enforcement Technology,* March 31, 2010.

25. Jacquelyn C. Campbell, Daniel W. Webster, and Nancy Glass, "The Danger Assessment Validation of a Lethality Risk Assessment Instrument for Intimate Partner Femicide," *Journal of Interpersonal Violence* 24, no. 4 (2009): 653-674.

26. Kanable, "Learning to Read the Danger Signs."

27. Ibid.

28. "Maryland Network Against Domestic Violence Wins Celebrating Solutions Award: Lethality Assessment Program-Maryland Model Recognized by the Mary Byron Project," Maryland Network Against Domestic Violence, accessed December 19, 2010, http://www.mnadv.org/news.html.

29. Kanable, "Learning to Read the Danger Signs."

30. "Murder of Tiana Notice Investigative Report—September 2010," State of Connecticut Officer of the Victim Advocate, accessed December 20, 2010, http://www.ct.gov/ova/lib/ova/notice_report_9_24_10.pdf.

31. Christine Dempsey, "Domestic Violence Victim's Father Helps Others By Buying, Installing Cameras," *The Hartford Courant,* December 10, 2010.

32. "Events," Tiana Angelique Notice Memorial Foundation, accessed December 20, 2010, http://tiananoticefoundation.org/?page_id=282.

33. Keith Rugar, "Family, Friends of Tiana Notice Rally in Her Honor," *The Informer,* February 18, 2010.

34. Celena Roby, e-mail discussions.

Four: The Producer

1. Peter Samuelson, "Everyone Deserves a Roof!" *The Huffington Post* (blog), December 11, 2008, http://www.huffingtonpost.com/peter-samuelson /everyone-deserves-a-roof_b_150131.html.
2. Martha Groves, "Upgrading From a Cardboard Box for the Homeless," *Los Angeles Times,* December 10, 2008.
3. "L.A.: Everyone Deserves a Roof," The Jay & Rose Phillips Family Foundation, accessed December 28, 2010, http://www.phillipsfnd.org /UploadFile/20/Spring%202010%20Newsletter.pdf.
4. "Homelessness & Poverty in America," National Law Center on Homelessness & Poverty, accessed December 28, 2010, http: //www.nlchp.org /hapia.cfm.
5. "The 2010 Annual Homeless Assessment Report," U.S. Department of Housing and Urban Development, accessed November 2, 2011, http: //www.hudhre.info/documents/2010HomelessAssessmentReport.pdf.
6. "Hunger and Homelessness Survey: A Status Report on Hunger and Homelessness in America's Cities," The United States Conference of Mayors, accessed December 28, 2010, http://www.usmayors.org /pressreleases/uploads/2010_Hunger-Homelessness_Report-final%20Dec %2021%202010.pdf.
7. Sudeep Reddy, "Downturn's Ugly Trademark: Steep, Lasting Drop in Wages," *The Wall Street Journal,* January 11, 2011.
8. "The State of the Nation's Housing," The Joint Center for Housing Studies of Harvard University, accessed January 3, 2011, http: //www.jchs.harvard.edu/sites/jchs.harvard.edu/files/son2011.pdf.
9. Ibid.
10. "Hunger and Homelessness Survey."
11. Jason Adam Wasserman and Jeffrey Michael Clair, *At Home on the Street: People, Poverty, and a Hidden Culture of Homelessness* (Boulder, CO: Lynne Rienner, 2010), 1.
12. Ibid.
13. University of Alabama at Birmingham, "At Home on the Street: First-Person Look At Homelessness," news release, January 21, 2010, http://main.uab.edu/Sites/MediaRelations/articles/72811/.
14. John Davis, "On the Streets: Why Homeless People Refuse Shelter," *Texas Tech Today,* accessed January 4, 2011, http://today.ttu.edu/2010 /01/on-the-streets-why-homeless-people-refuse-shelter/.
15. "L.A.: Everyone Deserves a Roof."

16. Groves, "Upgrading From a Cardboard Box for the Homeless."
17. "L.A.: Everyone Deserves a Roof."
18. Peter Samuelson (founder, EDAR), in telephone and e-mail discussions with the author, January 2011.
19. "L.A.: Everyone Deserves a Roof."
20. Pathways to Housing, *Annual Report 2007,* accessed January 11, 2011, http://www.pathwaystohousing.org/files/AnnualReport_2007.pdf.
21. David Bornstein, "A Plan to Make Homelessness History," *The New York Times,* December 20, 2010.
22. "Our Results," 100,000 Homes, accessed July 22, 2011, http://100khomes.org/our-results.
23. Bornstein, "A Plan to Make Homelessness History."
24. "L.A.: Everyone Deserves a Roof."
25. Groves, "Upgrading From a Cardboard Box for the Homeless."
26. Peter Samuelson, telephone and e-mail discussions.
27. Ibid.
28. Mark Foreman, *Wholly Jesus: His Surprising Approach to Wholeness and Why It Matters Today,* (Boise, ID: Ampelon, 2008), 205.

Five: The Hunger Heroes

1. "People, Projects, and Publications 2010-2011," The Committee on National Statistics, accessed February 1, 2011, http://www7.nationalacademies.org/cnstat/CNSTAT%20Brochure.pdf.
2. Mark Nord, Max Finberg, and James McLaughlin, "What Should the Government Mean by *Hunger?*" *Journal of Hunger & Environmental Nutrition* 4, no. 1 (2009): 20-47.
3. Patricia Allen, "The Disappearance of Hunger in America," *Gastronomica* 7, no. 3 (2007): 19-23.
4. Nord, Finberg, and McLaughlin, "What Should the Government Mean by *Hunger?*"
5. Frank I. Luntz, *Words That Work: It's Not What You Say, It's What People Hear* (New York: Hyperion, 2007), 164-169.
6. George McGovern, introduction to *Let Them Eat Promises: The Politics of Hunger in America,* by Nick Kotz (Garden City, NY: Anchor Books, 1968).
7. Allen, "The Disappearance of Hunger in America."
8. Alisha Coleman-Jensen et al., "Household Food Security in the United States in 2010," U.S. Department of Agriculture Economic Research Service, accessed November 2, 2011, http://www.ers.usda.gov/Publications/ERR125/ERR125.pdf.

9. Ibid.

10. James Mabli et al., "Hunger in America 2010: National Report Prepared for Feeding America," Mathematica Policy Research, January 2010, http://feedingamerica.org/faces-of-hunger/hunger-in-america-2010 /hunger-report-2010.aspx.

11. Feeding America, "New Report: More Than 49 Million Americans at Risk of Hunger," news release, November 16, 2009.

12. Adam B. Ellick, "The Chicken and Rice Man," *The New York Times,* November 25, 2007.

13. Ellick, "The Chicken and Rice Man."

14. "Why Sharing is a Beautiful Thing," *CNN Heroes,* accessed February 7, 2011, http://www.cnn.com/2010/OPINION/10/28/munoz.sharing /index.html.

15. Ellick, "The Chicken and Rice Man."

16. "Selected Social Characteristics in the United States: 2009, Queens County, New York," U.S. Census Bureau, accessed February 8, 2011, http://factfinder.census.gov/servlet/ADPTable?_bm=y&-geo_id =05000US36081&-context=adp&-ds_name=ACS_2009_1YR_G00_&- tree_id=309&-_lang=en&-_caller=geoselect&-format=.

17. Ellick, "The Chicken and Rice Man."

18. "Bus Driver Delivers Free Home-Cooked Meals," *CNN Living,* accessed February 7, 2011, http://articles.cnn.com/2009-03-19/living/cnnheroes .jorge.munoz_1_hot-meal-bus-driver-food?_s=PM:LIVING.

19. Clem Richardson, "The True Angel of Queens Fills Bellies of Hungry Day Workers Every Night," *New York Daily News,* December 11, 2009.

20. Ellick, "The Chicken and Rice Man."

21. "Why Sharing is a Beautiful Thing."

22. "2010 Year in Review," *Yahoo! News,* accessed February 8, 2011, http: //yearinreview.yahoo.com/2010/us_inspiring_acts#7phoebes-food-bank.

23. Christie Garton, "Act of Kindness at Trader Joe's Sparks Outpouring of Charitable Support on Facebook," *USA Today,* August 25, 2010.

24. "Carolee Hazard's 93 Dollar Club," Second Harvest Food Bank of Santa Clara and San Mateo Counties, accessed February 9, 2011, http://www .shfb.org/93dollarclub.

25. Stephen Clissold, *The Wisdom of St. Francis and His Companions,* (New York: New Directions, 1978), 28.

Six: The Kentuckian

1. "Leprosy (Hansen's Disease): What Is Leprosy," National Institute of

Allergy and Infectious Diseases, accessed February 15, 2011, http://www.niaid.nih.gov/topics/leprosy/Understanding/Pages/whatis.aspx.

2. "Leprosy (Hansen's Disease): History of the Disease," National Institute of Allergy and Infectious Diseases, accessed February 15, 2011, http://www.niaid.nih.gov/topics/leprosy/Understanding/Pages/history.aspx#.

3. Valerie Martin, *Salvation: Scenes from the Life of St. Francis* (New York: Alfred A. Knopf, 2001), 238-241.

4. Ibid.

5. "Hansen's Disease Treatment," National Park Service, accessed March 5, 2011, http://www.nps.gov/archive/kala/docs/hansens2.htm.

6. David U. Himmelstein et al., "Medical Bankruptcy in the United States, 2007: Results of a National Study," *The American Journal of Medicine* 122, no. 8 (2009): 741-746.

7. "Employer Health Benefits 2011 Annual Survey," The Kaiser Family Foundation and Health Research & Educational Trust, accessed November 2, 2011, http://ehbs.kff.org/pdf /2011/8225.pdf.

8. Himmelstein et al., "Medical Bankruptcy in the United States."

9. Greg Hitt and Janet Adamy, "House Passes Historic Health Bill," *The Wall Street Journal,* March 22, 2010.

10. Tom Brown, "Judge Strikes Down Healthcare Reform Law," *Reuters,* January 31, 2011, http://www.reuters.com/article/2011/01/31/us-usa-healthcare-ruling-idUSTRE70U6RY20110131?pageNumber=1.

11. Randy E. Barnett, "Is Health-Care Reform Constitutional?" *The Washington Post,* March 21, 2010.

12. Brown, "Judge Strikes Down Healthcare Reform Law."

13. Malcolm Gladwell, "The Moral Hazard Myth," *The New Yorker,* August 29, 2005.

14. Himmelstein et al., "Medical Bankruptcy in the United States."

15. "Health, United States, 2010: With Special Feature on Death and Dying," National Center for Health Statistics, accessed February 17, 2011, http://www.cdc.gov/nchs/data/hus/hus10.pdf.

16. Andrew P. Wilper et al., "Health Insurance and Mortality in U.S. Adults," *American Journal of Public* 99, no. 12 (2009): 2289-2295.

17. Leslie Askew, "Sunday Offering: Surgery For The Needy," Articles.CNN.com, accessed March 6, 2011, http://articles.cnn.com /2010-03-04/health/cnnheroes.sunday.surgery_1_plastic-surgeon-health-care-health-insurance?_s=PM:HEALTH.

18. Catherine Cole and Jessica Hopper, "Person of the Week: Surgery on Sunday Doctors Give Free Health Care to the Uninsured," ABCNews.com, accessed March 6, 2011, http://abcnews.go.com/WN /surgery-sunday-doctors-provide-free-surgeries-uninsured-receive/story?id =11180307.

19. Ibid.
20. Andy Moore (founder, Surgery on Sunday), in e-mail discussions with the author, March 2011.
21. Cole and Hopper, "Person of the Week."
22. Askew, "Sunday Offering: Surgery For The Needy."
23. Andy Moore, e-mail discussions.
24. Ibid.
25. Askew, "Sunday Offering: Surgery For The Needy."
26. Gerald F. Riley, "The Cost of Eliminating the 24-Month Medicare Waiting Period for Social Security Disabled-Worker Beneficiaries," *Medical Care* 42, no. 4 (2004): 387-394.
27. Andy Moore, e-mail discussions.
28. Cole and Hopper, "Person of the Week."
29. Parija B. Kavilanz, "Rx for Money Woes: Doctors Quit Medicine," CNNMoney.com, accessed March 15, 2011, http://money.cnn.com /2009/09/14/news/economy/health_care_doctors_quitting/index.htm.
30. Mark V. Pauly, "The Economics of Moral Hazard: Comment," *The American Economic Review* 58, no. 3 (1968): 531-537.
31. Gladwell, "The Moral Hazard Myth."

Seven: The Kid Saver

1. Tytti Solantaus, Jenni Leinonen, and Raija-Leena Punamäki, "Children's Mental Health in Times of Economic Recession: Replication and Extension of the Family Economic Stress Model in Finland," *Developmental Psychology* 40, no. 3 (2004): 412-429.
2. Seppo Honkapohja and Erkki Koskela, "The Economic Crisis of the 1990s in Finland," *Economic Policy* 14, no. 29 (1999): 399-436.
3. Tytti Solantaus, Jenni Leinonen, and Raija-Leena Punamäki, "Children's Mental Health in Times of Economic Recession."
4. Rand D. Conger and Glen H. Elder, Jr., *Families in Troubled Times: Adapting to Change in Rural America* (Hawthorne, New York: Aldine de Gruyter, 1994), 6-15.
5. Ibid.
6. Tytti Solantaus, Jenni Leinonen, and Raija-Leena Punamäki, "Children's Mental Health in Times of Economic Recession."
7. Kenneth C. Land, "2010 Child Well-Being Index (CWI)," Foundation for Child Development, accessed March 24, 2011, http://www.fcd-us.org/sites/default /files/FINAL%202010%20CWI%20Annual %20Release.pdf.
8. Carmen DeNavas-Walt, Bernadette D. Proctor, and Jessica C. Smith,

"Income, Poverty, and Health Insurance Coverage in the United States: 2010," U.S. Census Bureau, accessed November 5, 2011, http://www.census.gov /prod/2011pubs/p60-239.pdf.

9. Land, "2010 Child Well-Being Index."
10. DeNavas-Walt, Proctor, and Smith, "Income, Poverty, and Health Insurance Coverage in the United States: 2010."
11. Erik Eckholm, "Recession Raises Poverty Rate to a 15-Year High," *The New York Times,* September 17, 2010.
12. Land, "2010 Child Well-Being Index."
13. "Mom is Charged With Leaving 2 Kids on CTA Train," *Chicago Tribune,* January 1, 2008.
14. David Anderson, "Unleashing the Family: Safe Families for Vulnerable Children (Lydia Home)," in *A Heart for the Community: New Models for Urban and Suburban Ministry,* ed. John Fuder and Noel Castellanos (Chicago: Moody Publishers, 2009), 419.
15. "Child Maltreatment in Foster Care: CWLA Best Practice Guidelines," Child Welfare League of America, accessed May 23, 2011, http://www .hunter.cuny.edu/socwork/nrcfcpp/downloads/policy-issues/maltreatment-guidelines.pdf.
16. "Foster Care Statistics 2009," U.S. Department of Health and Human Services: Child Welfare Information Gateway, accessed May 20, 2011, http://www.childwelfare.gov/pubs/factsheets/foster.pdf.
17. "David Anderson," Ashoka United States, accessed May 27, 2011, http://usa.ashoka.org/danderson.
18. David Anderson (founder, Safe Families for Children), in telephone discussions with the author, May 2011.
19. "FAQ," Safe Families for Children, accessed May 27, 2011, http: //www.safe-families.org/whatis_faq.aspx.
20. David Anderson, telephone discussions.
21. "Protecting the Weakest: The Recession May Hurt American's Vulnerable Children," *The Economist,* February 25, 2010.
22. Lisa Black, "Chicago Parents in Crisis: Extended Child Care Proves a Godsend," *Chicago Tribune,* May 10, 2010.
23. Land, "2010 Child Well-Being Index."
24. Michele Ver Ploeg et al., "Access to Affordable and Nutritious Food: Measuring and Understanding Food Deserts and Their Consequences," U.S. Department of Agriculture Economic Research Service, accessed April 16, 2011, http://www.ers.usda.gov/Publications/AP/AP036/AP036 .pdf.
25. "David Anderson."
26. "History," Lydia Home Association, accessed May 30, 2011, http: //www.lydiahome.org/10086/content/content_id/9418/History.

27. David Anderson, telephone discussions.

28. David Steves, "Bill Seeks Safe Haven for Kids," *The Register-Guard,* February 5, 2010.

29. Drucker Institute, "Winners Chosen for the 2010 Drucker Award for Nonprofit Innovation," press release, October 10, 2010, http://www.druckerinstitute.com/link/winners-chosen-for-the-2010-drucker-award-for-nonprofit-innovation/.

30. Vincent Pierri, "Suburban Agency Places Children in Short-Term Foster Care," *Daily Herald,* December 27, 2009.

31. Danielle Hester, "An Alternative to DCFS," *The Chicago Reporter,* September 16, 2007.

32. Ibid.

Eight: The Second-Coat Givers

1. Anne Macdonell, *Sons of Francis* (New York: G.P. Putnam's Sons, 1902), 32.

2. Robin Gill, *A Textbook of Christian Ethics,* 3rd ed. (New York: T&T Clark, 2006), 140.

3. Wharton School, "Sharing the Wealth: Leonard Abess and the $60 Million Gift to His Employees," knowledge@wharton.com (April 29, 2009), http://knowledge.wharton.upenn.edu/article.cfm ?articleid=2228.

4. "Banker in Obama Speech Recognized for his Generosity," Articles.CNN.com, accessed June 29, 2011, http://articles.cnn.com /2009-02-24/politics/obama.guests_1_first-lady-abess-michelle-obama?s =PM:POLI-TICS.

5. Wharton School, "Sharing the Wealth."

6. Matt Krantz and Barbara Hansen, "CEO Pay Soars While Workers' Pay Stalls," *USA Today,* April 4, 2011.

7. Ibid.

8. Joann S. Lublin, "Executive Bonuses Bounce Back," *The Wall Street Journal,* March 18, 2011.

9. Ryan Dezember, "Transocean Regrets 'Insensitive' Wording in Filing," *The Wall Street Journal,* April 4, 2011.

10. Andrew M. Cuomo, "No Rhyme or Reason: The 'Heads I Win, Tails You Lose' Bank Bonus Culture," Attorney General State of New York, accessed June 29, 2011, http://www.oag.state.ny.us/media_center/2009 /july/pdfs/Bonus%20Report%20Final%207.30.09.pdf.

11. Robert B. Reich, *Aftershock: The Next Economy and America's Future* (New York: Alfred A. Knopf, 2010), 6-7.

12. Timothy Noah, "The United States of Inequality," Slate, September 3, 2010, http://www.slate.com/id/2266025/entry/2266026.
13. Hans C. Breiter et al., "Functional Imaging of Neural Responses to Expectancy and Experience of Monetary Gains and Losses," *Neuron* 30, no. 2 (2001): 619-639.
14. Jennifer Robison, "In Praise of Praising Your Employees," *Gallup Management Journal,* November 9, 2006, http://gmj.gallup.com/content /25369 /praise-praising-your-employees.aspx.
15. Ibid.
16. Tony Schwartz, "Greedy Bankers Are Like Coke Fiends," *AlterNet* (blog), November 4, 2010, http://www.alternet.org/story/148749/greedy _bankers_are_like_coke_fiends?page=entire.
17. Allie Torgan, "Adoptive Mom Helps 'Give Birth' to 43 Families," *CNN Heroes,* accessed July 8, 2011, http://edition.cnn.com/2011/US/05/19 /cnnheroes.becky.fawcett/.
18. "Board of Directors," Helpusadopt.org, accessed July 8, 2011, http: //www.helpusadopt.org/board.html.
19. "'Life-Changing' Grants Help Families Afford Adoption," *CNN Heroes,* accessed July 8, 2011, http://www.cnn.com/2011/US/05/24/cnnheroes .fawcett.adoption.extra/index.html.
20. Becky Fawcett (co-founder, Helpusadopt.org), in e-mail discussions with the author, July 2011.
21. Torgan, "Adoptive Mom Helps 'Give Birth' to 43 Families."
22. Ibid.
23. Becky Fawcett, e-mail discussions.
24. Ibid.
25. Denise Cox, "The Story," Denise Cox Designs, accessed July 13, 2011, http://www.denisecoxdesigns.com/story.html.
26. Ibid.
27. Leslie Gibson, "Rockwall's 'Foreclosure Samaritan' Gains National Spotlight," *Rockwall Herald Banner,* November 1, 2008.
28. "Introduction," Foreclosure Angel Foundation, accessed July 8, 2011, http://www.foreclosureangelfoundation.com/.
29. Glenn Ruppel and Justin Sturken, "Cash-Poor Americans Find Other Ways to Give," ABCNews.com, accessed July 8, 2011, http: //abcnews.go.com/2020/story?id=7866033&page=1.
30. Leslie Gibson, "Requests Pour In For RW's 'Foreclosure Angel,'" *Rockwall Herald Banner,* January 11, 2009.
31. Richard Abshire, "Rockwall Woman Still Saving Homes With Foreclosure Angel Foundation," Texas Cable News, http://www.txcn.com /sharedcontent/dws/news/localnews/stories/DN-foreclosure_28met.ART .State.Edition1.4bbbd90.html.

32. Noah Ovshinsky, "To Warm The Homeless, a Coat That's a Sleeping Bag," NPR, accessed July 9, 2011, http://www.npr.org/2010/12/13 /131910671/to-warm-the-homeless-a-coat-that-s-a-sleeping-bag.

33. Veronika Scott, "Frequently Asked Questions," *The Empowerment Plan* (blog), accessed July 9, 2011, http://detroitempowermentplan.blogspot .com/.

34. Michelle Nichols, "U.S. Billionaires Pledge Fortunes to Charity," *Reuters,* August 4, 2010, http://www.reuters.com/article/2010/08/04/us-wealth-philanthropy-billionaires-idUSTRE6733F520100804.

Nine: The Guardians of Animals

1. Father Candide Chalippe, *The Life and Legends of Saint Francis of Assisi* (London: The Echo Library, 2007), 276.

2. Linda Kalof, *Looking at Animals in Human History* (London: Reaktion Books, 2007), 68.

3. Virginia Halbur, ed., *Saint Mary's Press College Study Bible: New American Bible (*Winona, Minnesota: Saint Mary's Press, 2007), 19.

4. David Salter, *Holy and Noble Beasts: Encounters with Animals in Medieval Literature* (Rochester, NY: D. S. Brewer, 2001), 25-32.

5. Kalof, *Looking at Animals in Human History.*

6. Matthew Scully, *Dominion: The Power of Man, the Suffering of Animals, and the Call to Mercy* (New York: St. Martin's Press, 2002), *xi-xii.*

7. Sharon L. Peters, "Foreclosures Slam Doors on Pets, Too," *USA Today,* July 9, 2008.

8. Scully, *Dominion.*

9. John Whipple Dwinelle, *The Colonial History of the City of San Francisco* (Carlisle, MA: Applewood Books, 2011), 26.

10. Elaine Vitone, "Left Behind: Pets Abandoned in Foreclosure," *Ladies' Home Journal,* June 2009.

11. Ibid.

12. "Pet Statistics," American Society for the Prevention of Cruelty to Animals, accessed August 10, 2011, http://www.aspca.org/about-us/about-the-aspca.aspx.

13. Joshua M. Frank and Pamela Carlisle-Frank, "Companion Animal Overpopulation: Trends and Results of Major Efforts to Reach a 'No-Kill' Nation," paper presented at Annual Meeting of the American Sociological Association, Atlanta, GA, August 2003, http://www.firepaw.org/cao .PDF.

14. "About No Kill," PAWS Chicago, accessed August 12, 2011, http: //www.pawschicago.org /animal-advocacy/about-no-kill/.

15. Frank and Carlisle-Frank, "Companion Animal Overpopulation."
16. Michele Armstrong (founder, Lulu's Rescue), in telephone and e-mail discussions with the author, August 2011.
17. Amanda Cregan, "A New Breed of Dog Rescue," *The Intelligencer,* July 11, 2011.
18. Michele Armstrong, telephone and e-mail discussions.
19. Ibid.
20. Sharon L. Peters, "Pilots Fly Doomed Dogs to Better Life," *USA Today,* November 25, 2008.
21. Michele Armstrong, telephone and e-mail discussions.

Ten: Living Franciscanomics

1. Joan Mueller, *Francis: The Saint of Assisi* (New York: New City Press, 2010), 84-86.
2. Sophie Jewett, *God's Troubadour: The Story of Saint Francis of Assisi* (New York: Thomas Y. Crowell, 1910), 53-57.
3. Peter Samuelson (founder, EDAR), in telephone and e-mail discussions with the author, January 2011.
4. Michele Armstrong (founder, Lulu's Rescue), in telephone and e-mail discussions with the author, August 2011.
5. Mark Stelzner (founder, JobAngels), in e-mail discussions with the author, September 2010.
6. D. Andrew Austin and Mindy R. Levit, "The Debt Limit: History and Recent Increases," Congressional Research Service, August 3, 2011, http://www.fas.org/sgp/crs/misc/RL31967.pdf.
7. Damian Paletta and Matt Phillips, "S&P Strips U.S. of Top Credit Rating," *The Wall Street Journal,* August 6, 2011.
8. "No Thanks To Anyone: America Has Avoided Default, But Political Dysfunction is Threatening Its Chances of Economic Recovery," *The Economist,* August 6, 2011.
9. Graham Bowley, "Stocks Suffer Sharpest Drop Since 2008," *The New York Times,* August 7, 2011.
10. Sudeep Reddy and Ben Casselman, "Economic Signals Heighten Worries of a Double-Dip," *The Wall Street Journal,* September 23, 2011.
11. Ezra Klein, "Who Are The 99 Percent," *Wonkblog* (blog), October 4, 2011, http://www.washingtonpost.com/blogs/ezra-klein/post/who-are-the-99-percent/2011/08/25 /gIQAt87jKL_blog.html.

Index